Beyond Graduation

From disability to ABILITY

Dr. Tara Cosco, Editor

The mission of the book series, **From Disability to ABILITY**, is to present books on special education that inspire, support, and instill best practices in the field. Educators, parents, family, friends, and those with exceptionalities can acquire information, encouragement, and strategies that promote positive outcomes for everyone. The series will support educators in the field who may have students in their classroom who learn and interact with others differently. Teachers seeking help knowing how to work with challenging behaviors, neurodiverse students, meeting diverse academic needs, and ensuring effective inclusion practices can acquire knowledge and best practices from the series. Parents, family, friends, and those who learn differently will also find practical suggestions to support, advocate, and encourage others or yourself.

Books in the Series

Adapt & Thrive: Strategies for Inclusive and Special Education
by Tara Cosco (2026)

Beyond Graduation: Navigating Postsecondary Success for Students With Disabilities
by Antonio Ellis (2026)

Case Studies for Special Education Law: One Foot in the Real World the Other Grounded in the Law
by Michael Shaffer and Linda Dowell (2026)

I Think My Child Learns Differently: Black Parents, Disability, Special Education and Educational Advocacy
by Rona Frederick (2026)

Faith, Family, and Neurodiversity: Islamic Approaches to Understanding Autism
by Sadia Warsi and Sophia Memon (2026)

Editor's biography

Dr. Tara Cosco is an Associate Professor of Education in the Department of Teaching and Leading at Augusta University. She has a Bachelor of Arts degree in Elementary Education, a Master of Arts degree in Special Education, and a Doctoral Degree in Online Learning and Technology. Her educational licenses include Elementary Education K-5, Interventionist K-8, Interventionist 6-12, and Instructional Leader. Dr. Cosco began her career teaching elementary special education. She has taught in private and public schools, as well as in higher education. Her passion is helping teachers design effective lessons for all students and creating lifelong learners. If you have a proposal that you wish to have considered for publication in the series, please send a full prospectus and CV to Dr. Tara Cosco at TCOSCO@augusta.edu.

ADVANCE PRAISE FOR

Beyond Graduation

Navigating Postsecondary Success for Students With Disabilities

"*Beyond Graduation* is a transformative call to action for educators, families, and advocates committed to equity in postsecondary transition. Grounded in lived experience and rigorous research, this book confronts ableism, centers intersectionality, and offers practical, justice-driven strategies to support students with disabilities as they navigate life beyond high school. An essential read for anyone working to ensure that access, belonging, and opportunity are not privileges, but guaranteed rights."

Dr. Andraé Townsel
Superintendent
Calvert County Public Schools
President, National Alliance of Black School Educators (NABSE)

"This timely and compelling work redefines what it means to support students with disabilities beyond high school. Drawing on lived experience, powerful narratives, and justice-driven research, Dr. Antonio L. Ellis offers a bold vision for equitable postsecondary transition. Educators, families, and advocates will find both inspiration and practical tools to dismantle ableism and foster true inclusion. With clarity, compassion, and urgency, this book challenges institutions to move beyond compliance and toward transformation. It's essential reading for anyone committed to ensuring that opportunity, dignity, and belonging are guaranteed, not granted, for all students."

Ashlie Jones
Director of Postsecondary Transition
District of Columbia Public Schools

"As a professional who has worked in teacher preparation and the field of special education and transition since the early days of Supported Work in the 1980's, I can tell you that Dr. Ellis's unique focus on the intersection and layered impact of race, disability, and socioeconomic status on effective transition and postsecondary education for students with disabilities has been much needed and provides a missing lens of critical inquiry on this issue."

Dr. Elizabeth Altieri
Professor Emeritus
Radford University School of Teacher Education and Leadership

"Dr. Ellis has written a profound, must-read book for those seeking to be more effective in special education and transition. This unique, visionary, and timely book focuses on equity-focused and culturally responsive transition for students with disabilities. Each chapter is substantive and compelling in addressing challenges and needs, along with impactful recommendations and resources. I highly recommend it for families, practitioners, and P-12 and higher education professionals. You will not be disappointed."

Dr. Donna Y. Ford
Distinguished Professor of Education and Human Ecology
The Ohio State University

"Dr. Antonio Ellis is a consummate professional in the field of special education. This scholar-activist has dedicated his career to improving quality of life for children and young adults with special needs. He is particularly focused on children and young adults who are from traditionally underserved communities. All his earlier publications are exemplary illustrations of his expertise and deep commitment to improve learning opportunities for students in special education. This book is his yet another contribution that draws attention to a crucial aspect of special educational intervention, namely transition from schools to higher educational institutions. Mindful planning and methodical implementation of step-by-step guidance to special education students are key to their successful transition to higher education or the world of work. More importantly, sensitivity to the cultural, social, and economic aspects of the students is critical for successful outcomes of transition. Dr. Ellis has most comprehensively conceived and authored this book so that it can become a valuable resource for special education personnel in schools, university faculty, researchers, and parents of children with special needs."

Dr. Rc Saravanabhavan
Professor Emeritus
Howard University School of Education

Beyond Graduation

Navigating Postsecondary Success for Students With Disabilities

BY Antonio L. Ellis

FOREWORD BY Gloria Ladson-Billings

AFTERWORD BY Arne Duncan

Gorham, Maine

Published by Myers Education Press, LLC
P.O. Box 424
Gorham, ME 04038

Myers Education Press is an academic publisher specializing in books, e-books, and digital content in the field of education. All of our books are subjected to a rigorous peer review process and produced in compliance with the standards of the Council on Library and Information Resources.

Library of Congress Cataloging-in-Publication Data available from Library of Congress.

13-digit ISBN 978-1-9755-0945-3 (paperback)
13-digit ISBN 978-1-9755-0946-0 (library networkable e-edition)
13-digit ISBN 978-1-9755-0946-0 (consumer e-edition)

Printed in the United States of America.

All first editions printed on acid-free paper that meets the American National Standards Institute Z39-48 standard.

Books published by Myers Education Press may be purchased at special quantity discount rates for groups, workshops, training organizations, and classroom usage. Please call our customer service department at 1-800-232-0223 for details.

Cover design by Teresa Lagrange.

Visit us on the web at **www.myersedpress.com** to browse our complete list of titles.

DEDICATION

To my own resilience, as a Black man with a stuttering disability who navigated the path to postsecondary life without the benefit of a transition plan. This book is a testament to the journey of becoming a rose that grew from concrete, watered by perseverance, faith, and purpose.

And to every child with a disability across the world: May the pages of this book serve as a beacon of possibility, paving a more just and inclusive pathway than the one I was given, and continue to walk.

CONTENTS

FIGURES AND TABLES

Figures

Tables

ACKNOWLEDGEMENTS

This book is dedicated to the students with disabilities I had the honor of serving during my 20 years with the District of Columbia Public Schools. Your resilience, brilliance, and perseverance have profoundly shaped my understanding of what it means to advocate, educate, and lead with compassion and justice.

I am equally grateful to the children I support each week through the Kid's Street Inclusion Ministry at Alfred Street Baptist Church in Alexandria, Virginia. Your presence continues to remind me that inclusion is not just a strategy, but a spiritual and moral imperative.

To my colleagues around the world who engage with and uplift my scholarship, thank you. Your encouragement, collaboration, and shared commitment to equity in education sustain this work and keep it moving forward.

FOREWORD

GLORIA LADSON-BILLINGS

In the mid-20th century, students with disabilities were an afterthought in public education. Public Law 94-142, the Education for All Handicapped Children Act, had not been passed and the fate of students with disabilities was severely limited. In many contexts, students with disabilities were cordoned off in basement-level classrooms where they participated in rote and menial tasks like coloring and assembling puzzles. In another set of contexts, students with disabilities are fully segregated in special schools that cater to their specific disabilities. In a third context, students with disabilities were fully invisible because they remain sequestered in their homes, receiving no educational support, spending every day being tended by parents and/or other caregivers. However, the enactment of PL 94-142 brought a new population into public schools across the country. And despite integrating students with disabilities into the PK-12 arena, their place in higher education has been less clear.

I once visited a university in a rural part of South Africa, and during a visit to the countryside we stopped in a small community that had been a township during the tragedy known as apartheid. This township, "Qwa Qwa," reminded me of every Black community I have ever visited. There are barbers and braiders sprinkled throughout the community along with small restaurants and businesses along the main streets. On the previous Sunday I had attended church in the community and got to know some of the local leaders. However, on one particular day I was invited to visit a house where a group of grandmothers had organized a program for students with disabilities. When I arrived, I was bombarded by students who seemed to be between the ages of 12 and 25. They were eager to introduce themselves, shake my hand, learn my name, and know where I was from. Hearing that I was from the United States brought a chorus of oohs and aahs. When I began talking with the grandmothers, I learned that their effort came about because they noticed that daily when the school buses departed after having picked up the school-aged students, the students with disabilities remained at home with nothing to do. So, the grandmothers of the community decided they needed to do something. During the week they assemble the students and plan a few activities for them. "We take them on picnics, to the zoo, or even to the beach since we know these are experiences they have never had," one of the grandmothers responded. South Africa has no PL 94-142. There is no requirement to educate students with disabilities, and yet, a group of community-minded elders know something must be done. These students are unlikely to attend college, but these grandmothers knew they needed something. The advantage of life in the United States is that college IS a possibility for students with disability—just not a guarantee.

Negotiating college is a challenge for all students. Being required to plan their schedules, choosing majors and courses, cultivating adult relationships, and figuring out career paths are but a few of the things collegiate students have to navigate. Imagine doing this with a disability and imagine doing it in a place that has no real understanding of how to assist and accommodate students with disabilities!

Some years ago, I was teaching a freshman seminar that attracted a large number of African American students. I recognized that most were first-generation students who, although quite bright—good grade point averages and good standardized test scores—were unfamiliar with college-going behavior. To help remedy some of their likely knowledge gaps, I insisted that coming to my office hours be a course requirement. For most of the students this requirement seems to be a punishment because in their high school experiences, going to see their teachers was something you did because you were in academic trouble. Students who were failing went to see their teachers. I had to explain to my students that their white peers regularly came to my office hours. They recognize that distinguishing themselves is one of the ways they are likely to get the benefit of the doubt when it comes to grades. Professors are people too, and in the midst of computing grades, actually knowing a student might spell the difference between a B-plus and an A-minus.

On one afternoon a young woman appeared at my office door and I welcomed her in. She smiled, walked in, and settled into the chair directly in front of my desk. I started with some perfunctory comments about how she was doing and adjusting to her new life as a college student. She seemed to enjoy being a college student and being at the state's premier institution had her entire family bragging. However, at one point she stopped talking and lowered her head. I allowed the silence to linger. "Professor," she began, "I'm having trouble keeping up with the reading." When I inquired as to what the problem with the reading might be she revealed that she had difficulty reading more than about 10 pages a day. I knew that would never do. There were certainly more than 10 pages a day to be read in my class, and she had three other classes. I explained to her that a 10-page-a-day strategy was not going to work at a highly competitive university.

I cleared my throat and asked if she had met with the staff at our campus disability resource center. She admitted that she had not. In fact, she was unaware that we even had such a place. I explained that her student fees covered the cost of the center and then rephrased in a way that I knew Black students, students who shared my background and college-going experience, would understand. "You are already paying for the service! You don't want to take advantage of it?" Knowing she would not want to waste money, she agreed to go to the center to inquire as to how they might help. Within 24 hours, the staff at the disability resource center reached out to me as one of the student's professors to get my syllabus and links for all of the course readings. In less than a week all of the student's instructors had been contacted and all of the course readings were audio-recorded. Four years later, I watched that young woman march proudly into the university's massive stadium to have her degree confirmed.

The abovementioned story is a success one. Unfortunately, most institutions of higher education do not have high rates of success for students with disabilities. The lack of academic as well as social-emotional supports and accommodations is evident despite the expressed commitment to serving students with disabilities. Most college/university professors and staff are programmed to serve students who are deemed "college-ready" and need no accommodations, but the reality of life in our nation is that human beings exist along a vast continuum of ability.

The work of 21st century institutions of higher education is to be flexible and nimble enough to meet the needs of students of all abilities and identities. Most have figured out how to make physical accommodations. The pavements have curb cuts. The buildings have door-openers and elevators. Most campuses allow service animals, and public presentations include sign language interpreters. But those accommodations may not be enough to ensure success for students with disabilities. Much of college success depends on what happens in the classroom and/or collegiate living in dormitories or other independent living environments.

In ideal higher educational settings, institutions plan and pursue missions and visions that may include statements of inclusivity. However, how that inclusivity is converted into action is regularly less than ideal. How many of our faculty carefully plan course syllabi with students with disabilities in mind? How many of our faculty engage in pedagogical practices that incorporate strategies that work for students with disabilities? How much of our campus programming is designed around issues of students with disabilities, not just so-called "regular" programs with accommodations?

Clearly, higher education can do a better job of weaving the perspectives and needs of students with disabilities into their overall understanding of what it means to educate *all* students. Of course, many of our students with disabilities also embrace other identities around race, ethnicity, class, gender, language, religion, and sexuality. How we move their concerns to the center of our planning and implementation is a strategy we have yet to master. We have to get past the notion of just "and," as in Black *and* disabled or working class *and* disabled or first generation *and* disabled. We need to prepare for students with disabilities as a primary way that they show up on our college and university campuses.

Gloria Ladson-Billings
Professor Emerita
University of Wisconsin-Madison

PART I

Understanding Postsecondary Transition

CHAPTER 1

The State of Transition for Students With Disabilities

Transition planning for students with disabilities represents one of the most critical junctures in the journey toward postsecondary success. As students near the completion of their secondary education, the shift to adulthood demands thoughtful preparation across multiple domains, including education, employment, and independent living. Despite the promises embedded within federal legislation such as the Individuals with Disabilities Education Act (IDEA, 2004), which mandates transition services beginning no later than age 16 (and earlier in some states), many students with disabilities continue to face significant barriers when navigating this pivotal stage (Mazzotti et al., 2021). In this chapter, I aim to explore the current state of transition services and outcomes, offering a foundation for reimagining supports that truly empower young people with disabilities beyond high school.

The statistics surrounding postsecondary outcomes for students with disabilities reveal a concerning reality. Data from the National Longitudinal Transition Study-2 (NLTS-2) demonstrate that youth with disabilities are less likely than their nondisabled peers to enroll in and complete postsecondary education, obtain competitive employment, and live independently (Newman et al., 2011). Although some progress has been made over the past two decades, these disparities persist, particularly for students from multiply marginalized backgrounds, including students of color and students from low-income communities who also experience disability (Gothberg et al., 2019). Through this chapter, I emphasize that systemic barriers, not individual limitations, are often at the heart of transition challenges, and addressing these inequities requires a broader, more critical lens.

Several factors contribute to the uneven landscape of transition success, including gaps in access to high-quality transition planning, limited availability of inclusive postsecondary programs, and ongoing employer bias in the labor market. Research continues to affirm that effective transition services are linked to early, individualized planning, meaningful student involvement, interagency collaboration, and the promotion of self-determination skills (Test et al., 2009). However, consistent implementation remains elusive, particularly in rural, urban, and under-resourced schools (Morningstar et al., 2017). I argue that until educational systems fully commit to providing equitable, strengths-based transition services, many students with disabilities will continue to graduate without the necessary supports to achieve their personal, academic, and professional aspirations.

In addition to institutional barriers, societal perceptions of disability profoundly shape transition experiences. Ableism, the systemic privileging of nondisabled norms, continues to influence educational settings, workforce development programs, and broader community life, often resulting in lowered expectations and diminished resources for students with disabilities (Annamma et al., 2013). In this chapter, I assert that dismantling ableist assumptions and centering disability as a valued aspect of human diversity are essential steps toward achieving more equitable postsecondary outcomes. When transition planning is grounded in students' strengths, identities, and ambitions rather than perceived deficits, it becomes a powerful tool for empowerment and systemic change.

By critically examining the current landscape of transition for students with disabilities, this chapter provides a lens to understand both the persistent barriers and the promising practices that exist today. I situate transition outcomes within broader social, economic, and political contexts, highlighting why the field must move beyond compliance-driven models toward holistic, student-centered, and justice-oriented approaches. My hope is that by confronting these realities, readers will gain a deeper appreciation for the work still needed, and the transformative possibilities ahead, for students with disabilities as they move beyond graduation.

Current Trends and Challenges

The field of transition services for students with disabilities is evolving in response to changing societal expectations, advances in disability rights advocacy, and greater attention to postsecondary outcomes. One notable trend is the growing emphasis on promoting self-determination and self-advocacy among students during the transition process. Research consistently shows that students who are actively involved in their transition planning, expressing preferences, setting goals, and participating in decision-making, experience better postsecondary outcomes in education, employment, and independent living (Test et al., 2009). Many transition programs now incorporate person-centered planning models and curricula designed to teach self-advocacy skills as a core component of preparing students for life after high school (Aleman-Tovar et al., 2022).

Another positive development is the expansion of inclusive postsecondary education (IPSE) programs for students with intellectual and developmental disabilities. These programs, often located on college and university campuses, provide opportunities for students to engage in academic coursework, vocational training, and campus life with appropriate supports (Ingram, 2013). The growth of IPSE initiatives reflects a broader societal commitment to educational access and inclusion, aligning with the principles outlined in the Higher Education Opportunity Act (2008). However, access to these programs remains uneven, and many students, particularly those from rural areas or under-resourced schools, encounter significant geographic and financial barriers to participation.

Despite these encouraging trends, serious challenges persist. One major concern is the inconsistency in the quality and implementation of transition services across states and school districts. Although IDEA mandates transition planning, the depth and effectiveness of these plans vary widely (Mazzotti et al., 2021). In many cases, transition planning remains a compliance-driven exercise rather than a dynamic, student-centered process. Furthermore, students with significant support needs, such as those with multiple disabilities, often receive less robust transition planning than their peers, perpetuating inequities in postsecondary opportunities (Plotner & Marshall, 2015). Addressing these inconsistencies requires sustained investment in professional development for educators and systemic accountability measures.

Adding to these concerns is the potential impact of proposals to eliminate the United States Department of Education. The department plays a critical role in enforcing federal laws like the Individuals with Disabilities Education Act and the Higher Education Opportunity Act, both of which contain essential provisions for transition planning and services. Without federal oversight and guidance, transition services could become even more inconsistent, with states and localities left to determine the extent of their commitment to supporting students with disabilities. Some states may maintain strong systems, while others could drastically reduce funding, remove accountability measures, or dismantle services entirely. Such an outcome would likely exacerbate existing disparities, leaving many students with disabilities vulnerable to inequitable practices and weakened protections during the transition to adulthood.

Employment outcomes remain another persistent challenge. Although gaining employment is a common postsecondary goal for many students with disabilities, data reveal significant gaps in labor force participation and earnings compared to nondisabled peers (Siperstein et al., 2013). Employers often express concerns about hiring individuals with disabilities due to misconceptions about productivity, accommodations, and workplace integration (Ju et al., 2013). Efforts to promote disability-inclusive hiring practices, expand supported employment services, and strengthen school-to-work partnerships are critical steps toward improving employment outcomes. Still, without addressing underlying societal biases and systemic discrimination, meaningful progress will remain limited.

Finally, transition planning continues to struggle with fully addressing the intersectionality of disability, race, ethnicity, gender, and socioeconomic status. Students of color with disabilities often face compounded barriers during transition, including lower expectations from educators, reduced access to rigorous coursework, and limited participation in transition planning meetings (Gothberg et al., 2019). Programs and policies that do not explicitly consider these intersecting forms of oppression risk perpetuating inequities rather than dismantling them. As shown in **Table 1.1**, these systemic trends reveal measurable gaps that require targeted, justice-focused responses at every level of policy and practice. Moving forward, transition services must adopt a culturally responsive and equity-centered lens that recognizes the full diversity of students' identities and experiences, ensuring that all young people with disabilities are prepared to navigate life beyond graduation with dignity, agency, and opportunity.

Table 1.1 – Systemic Barriers and Equity Implications in Postsecondary Transition for Students With Disabilities

Trend or Challenge	**Description**	**Implications for Equity**
Declining Transition Outcomes	Many students with disabilities experience lower rates of college enrollment and employment	Indicates the need for earlier, individualized, and culturally responsive transition planning
Inconsistent Implementation of IDEA	Transition mandates under IDEA vary widely across states and districts	Creates inequities in access to services and postsecondary preparation
Overemphasis on Compliance	Individualized Education Program (IEP) transition plans are often treated as paperwork rather than meaningful road maps	Reduces student engagement and limits personalization of postsecondary pathways
Ableist Definitions of "Readiness"	Readiness is often measured by standardized metrics that ignore systemic barriers	Excludes students whose strengths and needs fall outside narrow academic benchmarks
Intersectional Inequities	Race, socioeconomic status, and language background compound disability-related disparities	Requires schools to adopt intersectional, justice-centered approaches to transition support

The Need for a 21st Century Approach

The evolving demands of the 21st century require a transformative rethinking of how we prepare students with disabilities for life beyond high school. Traditional models of transition planning, often rooted in outdated assumptions about employment and independent living, no longer reflect the realities of today's global economy, technological advancements, and shifting social landscapes. To truly support postsecondary success, we must embrace an approach that moves beyond compliance and checklists and instead prioritizes innovation, student agency, and equity at every stage of the transition process.

Students with disabilities today navigate a world that is far more interconnected, diverse, and dynamic than previous generations experienced. The rise of remote work, digital platforms, and entrepreneurial opportunities has opened new possibilities that were once unimaginable. Yet, many transition plans continue to funnel students toward a narrow set of postsecondary options that fail to align with these emerging realities. A 21st century approach to transition must prepare students to be adaptable, technologically fluent, and empowered to forge individualized pathways that reflect their passions, talents, and identities.

Moreover, the future of work and community engagement demands critical thinking, collaboration, creativity, and resilience. Students with disabilities must be equipped not only with technical skills but also with the self-determination and confidence to advocate for themselves in complex and evolving environments. This requires a shift from a deficit-based perspective, one that focuses on what students cannot do, to a strengths-based framework that recognizes disability as a source of creativity, innovation, and leadership. Building environments that nurture these attributes is not a luxury; it is a necessity for ensuring that students with disabilities can thrive.

A 21st century approach also calls for a transition system that centers equity and inclusion, acknowledging the intersecting factors that shape students' experiences. Race, gender identity, socioeconomic status, geographic location, and language background all influence access to opportunities and supports. A truly modern transition framework must account for these complexities and commit to dismantling systemic barriers that have historically marginalized students with disabilities. Equity must be embedded not just in program goals but also in everyday practices, policies, and relationships with students and families.

Ultimately, preparing students with disabilities for the future means preparing them for full lives, lives rich with possibility, dignity, purpose, and connection. This vision demands that we reimagine transition planning as a dynamic, creative, and student-driven process, one that adapts to the rapid pace of societal change while holding firmly to the principles of justice and inclusion. The call for a 21st century approach is not simply about keeping up with the times; it is about recognizing the boundless potential of students with disabilities and ensuring that the systems surrounding them rise to meet that potential with boldness and compassion.

As we move forward, it becomes clear that reimagining transition services for the 21st century is not only necessary but urgent. Students with disabilities deserve pathways that honor their strengths, respect their aspirations, and prepare them for meaningful lives beyond graduation. This reimagining must begin early, long before students stand at the threshold of adulthood. In the next chapter, I will explore how transition planning in high school serves as a critical foundation for postsecondary success. By examining effective strategies, common pitfalls, and opportunities for innovation, I aim to highlight how early, intentional, and student-centered planning can transform possibilities for young people with disabilities as they navigate their futures.

References

Annamma, S. A., Connor, D., & Ferri, B. (2013). Dis/ability critical race studies (DisCrit): Theorizing at the intersections of race and dis/ability. *Race Ethnicity and Education, 16*(1), 1–31. https://doi.org/10.1080/13613324.2012.730511

Gothberg, J. E., Greene, G., & Kohler, P. D. (2019). District implementation of research-based practices for transition planning with culturally and linguistically diverse youth with disabilities and their families. *Career Development and Transition for Exceptional Individuals, 42*(2), 77–86.

Higher Education Opportunity Act of 2008, 20 U.S.C. § 1001 et seq.

Individuals with Disabilities Education Act of 2004, 20 U.S.C. § 1400 et seq.

Ingram, C. (2013). Think college: Postsecondary education options for students with intellectual disabilities. *Journal of Applied Rehabilitation Counseling, 44*(1), 49.

Ju, S., Roberts, E., & Zhang, D. (2013). Employer attitudes toward workers with disabilities: A review of research in the past decade. *Journal of Vocational Rehabilitation, 37*(1), 1–9. https://doi.org/10.3233/JVR-2012-0574

Mazzotti, V. L., Rowe, D. A., Kwiatek, S., Voggt, A., Chang, W. H., Fowler, C. H., ... & Test, D. W. (2021). Secondary transition predictors of postschool success: An update to the research base. *Career Development and Transition for Exceptional Individuals, 44*(1), 47-64.

Morningstar, M. E., Lombardi, A., Fowler, C. H., & Test, D. W. (2017). A college and career readiness framework for secondary students with disabilities. *Career Development and Transition for Exceptional Individuals, 41*(1), 45–55. https://doi.org/10.1177/2165143415589926

Newman, L., Wagner, M., Knokey, A. M., C.., Nagle, K., Shaver, D., & Wei, X. (2011). *The post-high school outcomes of young adults with disabilities up to 8 years after high school: A report from the National Longitudinal Transition Study-2 (NLTS2)* (NCSER 2011-3005). U.S. Department of Education.

Plotner, A. J., & Marshall, K. J. (2015). Postsecondary education programs for students with an intellectual disability: Facilitators and barriers to implementation. *Intellectual and Developmental Disabilities*, 53(1), 58–69. https://doi.org/10.1352/1934-9556-53.1.58

Raley, S. K., Shogren, K. A., Rifenbark, G. G., Lane, K. L., & Pace, J. R. (2021). The impact of the self-determined learning model of instruction on student self-determination in inclusive, secondary classrooms. *Remedial and special education, 42*(6), 363–373.

Siperstein, G. N., Parker, R. C., & Drascher, M. (2013). National snapshot of adults with intellectual disabilities in the labor force. *Journal of Vocational Rehabilitation, 41*(3), 165–178. https://doi.org/10.3233/JVR-140711

Test, D. W., Fowler, C. H., Richter, S. M., White, J., Mazzotti, V., Walker, A. R., & Kortering, L. (2009). Evidence-based practices in secondary transition. *Career Development for Exceptional Individuals, 32*(2), 115–128. https://doi.org/10.1177/0885728809336859

CHAPTER 2

Transition Planning in High School

For students with disabilities, transition planning must begin early, ideally by middle school and no later than the early years of high school, to maximize postsecondary success. Early planning provides students with the time and opportunities necessary to develop the skills, experiences, and supports they need to achieve their long-term goals. Research consistently shows that when transition services are initiated well before graduation, students have a greater likelihood of enrolling in postsecondary education, securing employment, and living independently (Beatson et al., 2023; Test et al., 2009). Beginning early also allows students to explore their interests, preferences, and strengths over time, leading to more informed and meaningful postsecondary pathways. Delayed or superficial transition planning, by contrast, often results in missed opportunities, rushed decision-making, and diminished post-school outcomes.

Transition planning should not be treated as a one-time event or a static task to be completed at a specific age. Rather, it must be understood as a dynamic, developmental process that evolves as students grow, mature, and refine their aspirations. Students' goals at age 14 are rarely identical to their goals at age 18, and effective transition planning must be flexible enough to adapt to these natural changes.

The Individuals with Disabilities Education Act (IDEA, 2004) reinforces this perspective by requiring that transition services be based on ongoing assessments of students' needs, strengths, preferences, and interests. High-quality transition planning continually engages students in reflecting on their experiences, adjusting their goals, and building the skills necessary for adulthood, ensuring that preparation for postsecondary life is comprehensive and responsive.

This chapter explores the foundational elements necessary for effective transition planning in high school and earlier. I begin by examining the legal and policy frameworks that govern transition services, with a particular focus on IDEA, the Rehabilitation Act, and the Americans with Disabilities Act. Understanding these mandates is essential because they define the rights of students with disabilities and set standards for educational systems to meet. From there, I turn to the core components of effective transition planning, including student-centered planning, family involvement, interagency collaboration, and the development of self-determination skills. These elements form the backbone of successful practices and must be intentionally integrated into all transition processes.

The chapter also addresses persistent challenges that undermine transition efforts. Despite federal mandates, there remains significant variability in the quality of transition services provided across states and districts (Beatson et al., 2023). Compliance-driven approaches, low expectations for students with disabilities, limited resources, and systemic inequities related to race, class, and language all continue to create barriers to effective planning (Aleman-Tovar & Burke, 2022). In particular, students from marginalized communities often face compounded obstacles that limit their access to high-quality transition services. Addressing these systemic issues is critical to ensuring that transition planning leads to genuine postsecondary opportunities rather than reproducing cycles of disadvantage.

In response to these barriers, I present best practices that can transform transition planning into a more empowering and equitable process. Drawing on research and promising models, I outline strategies such as starting transition conversations early, employing culturally responsive planning approaches, embedding transition goals across all areas of instruction, and prioritizing authentic student voice. These practices emphasize a strengths-based orientation, positioning students not as passive recipients of services but as active agents in shaping their futures. When implemented thoughtfully, they can radically shift the trajectory of students with disabilities toward outcomes marked by dignity, choice, and success.

Finally, throughout this chapter, I offer practical examples and reflections designed to bring these concepts to life. By grounding discussion in real-world practices and challenges, I aim to provide readers, whether they are educators, transition coordinators, families, or policymakers, with a deeper understanding of what meaningful transition planning entails. Preparing students for adulthood is not simply about meeting legal requirements; it is about honoring their aspirations, investing in their growth, and building systems that recognize and nurture their potential. Through this lens, transition planning becomes not just an educational obligation but an act of transformative justice.

The Legal and Policy Foundations of Transition Planning

Transition Requirements Under IDEA

IDEA (2004) fundamentally reshaped the landscape of transition planning for students with disabilities by establishing clear legal mandates for schools to prepare students for postsecondary life. According to IDEA, transition services must be included in a student's Individualized Education Program (IEP) beginning no later than age 16, though many states encourage starting earlier (IDEA, 2004, § 300.320(b)). These services are intended to be results oriented, focusing on improving academic and functional achievement to facilitate movement from school to postschool activities, including higher education, employment, and independent living. The law places the responsibility on schools to ensure that students are equipped with the necessary skills, experiences, and supports to successfully navigate adulthood.

A key feature of IDEA's transition mandates is the requirement for measurable postsecondary goals based on age-appropriate transition assessments related to education, employment, and, where appropriate, independent living skills (IDEA, 2004). These goals must be individualized to reflect the student's strengths, preferences, and interests, rather than being predetermined or standardized. Furthermore, the IEP must outline the transition services needed to assist the student in reaching those goals, including instruction, related services, community experiences, and the development of employment and other adult living objectives. In this way, transition planning under IDEA is designed to be an integrated and forward-thinking component of the overall educational experience.

IDEA also requires that students be actively involved in their transition planning process. Beginning at age 16, students must be invited to their own IEP meetings whenever transition services are discussed (IDEA, 2004, § 300.321(b)). This provision recognizes the importance of fostering self-determination and empowering students to articulate their aspirations and advocate for their needs. Additionally, with the consent of the parent or student (once the student reaches the age of majority), schools must invite representatives of any agencies likely to provide or pay for transition services, such as vocational rehabilitation agencies. This interagency collaboration is critical for creating seamless transitions from school-based services to adult systems of support.

While IDEA provides a strong framework for transition planning, its implementation across states and districts remains inconsistent. Some schools view transition requirements as merely a compliance issue, completing minimal paperwork to meet legal obligations without genuinely engaging students in meaningful planning (Beatson et al., 2023). To fulfill the true intent of IDEA, educators must move beyond procedural compliance and embrace transition planning as a vital, student-centered process that can open doors to autonomy, community participation, and lifelong success. Ensuring that transition planning under IDEA is both robust and authentic is essential to supporting the full potential of students with disabilities as they prepare to move beyond high school.

The IEP's Role in Transition Planning

The IEP serves as the central tool for shaping transition services for students with disabilities. As mandated by IDEA (2004), the IEP must include a coordinated set of activities that promote movement from school to postsecondary outcomes such as further education, employment, and independent living. Beginning no later than age 16 or earlier if determined appropriate, the IEP must contain measurable postsecondary goals based on age-appropriate transition assessments (IDEA, 2004, § 300.320(b)). These goals ensure that transition planning is individualized and that educational programs are aligned with the student's long-term aspirations rather than being driven solely by generic curricula.

The IEP team, which includes educators, the student, family members, and other relevant stakeholders, plays a crucial role in designing and implementing transition services. Transition planning within the IEP process requires collaboration across disciplines, bringing together expertise in academics, vocational training, counseling, and life skills development. Research shows that IEPs that clearly articulate students' preferences, strengths, and support needs are more likely to result in positive postsecondary outcomes (Test et al., 2009). A well-developed transition plan within the IEP acts as a road map, identifying the instructional activities, community experiences, and support services needed to help the student achieve their goals.

Student involvement in developing the IEP is particularly critical during transition planning. IDEA emphasizes that students must be invited to participate in any meeting where transition goals and services are discussed, promoting their voice and agency in the process (IDEA, 2004, § 300.321(b)). Engaging students meaningfully in their IEP development fosters self-determination skills, such as goal-setting, decision-making, and self-advocacy, that are essential for success in adulthood (Wehmeyer et al., 2012). When students are positioned as active contributors rather than passive recipients, the IEP becomes not just a legal document but a powerful tool for empowerment and future planning.

Despite the clear importance of transition planning within the IEP, challenges persist in practice. Some IEPs include transition services that are vague, generic, or disconnected from students' actual goals, reducing their effectiveness (Beatson et al., 2023). Additionally, educators often report a lack of training and resources to develop high-quality, individualized transition plans. To realize the full potential of the IEP in transition planning, school teams must prioritize early, ongoing, and student-centered planning processes, ensuring that every element of the IEP is intentionally aligned to support a successful transition to postsecondary life.

Key Themes in Transition Planning

Transition planning for students with disabilities is multifaceted, involving legal compliance, educational best practices, and a deep commitment to student-centered processes. This chapter highlights several critical themes that are essential for understanding how to develop effective transition plans. These themes include the legal and policy foundations of transition services, the core components of high-quality planning, the persistent barriers that students and educators face, and the promising practices that have emerged to address these challenges. By exploring these interconnected areas, I aim to provide a comprehensive guide to the complexities of transition planning in high school settings.

The chapter first examines the legal requirements that frame transition services, particularly the mandates outlined in IDEA (2004) and complementary legislation such as the Rehabilitation Act and the Americans with Disabilities Act. Understanding these frameworks is crucial, as they establish the rights of students with disabilities and set the minimum standards for educational practices. Without a solid grasp of the legal context, transition planning risks becoming either superficial or inequitable. By grounding the discussion in these legal foundations, this chapter emphasizes that transition services are not optional enhancements but federally protected rights.

Following the legal discussion, the chapter delves into the key components of effective transition planning, including student involvement, family engagement, interagency collaboration, and the development of self-determination skills. Each of these elements plays a pivotal role in helping students envision and realize their postsecondary goals (Test et al., 2009; Wehmeyer et al., 2012). Successful transition planning requires educators to coordinate supports across multiple systems, build authentic relationships with students and families, and create educational experiences that foster independence and resilience. These practices represent the gold standard for supporting students as they prepare for adulthood.

Finally, the chapter addresses both the barriers that impede transition planning and the best practices that offer solutions. Challenges such as inconsistent implementation, low expectations, systemic inequities, and limited resources continue to hinder progress (Aleman-Tovar & Burke, 2022; Beatson et al., 2023). However, innovative strategies, such as early and culturally responsive transition planning, authentic assessments, and student-led IEP meetings, have demonstrated the potential to transform outcomes. By identifying both obstacles and opportunities, this chapter underscores the need for transition planning that is not only legally compliant but also empowering, equitable, and genuinely responsive to the diverse aspirations of students with disabilities.

Legal and Policy Foundations of Transition Planning

Transition Mandates Under IDEA

IDEA (2004) serves as the cornerstone of federal protections for students with disabilities transitioning from secondary to postsecondary life. IDEA mandates that transition planning be included in the IEP by age 16, though earlier planning is recommended (IDEA, 2004, § 300.320(b)). These transition services are intended to be results oriented, designed to improve academic and functional achievement and facilitate movement to postschool activities such as higher education, employment, and independent living. This legislative requirement ensures that transition is not left to chance but is purposefully embedded within the educational experience.

A distinguishing feature of IDEA's transition mandates is the focus on individualized, measurable postsecondary goals based on age-appropriate assessments. These goals are not merely aspirational; they are actionable benchmarks intended to drive educational programming and services toward preparing students for real-world success. Schools must align services, coursework, and community experiences with these goals, making transition planning a central, guiding force in a student's secondary education. Without this legal requirement, transition services would likely remain fragmented and inconsistently applied.

Moreover, IDEA stipulates that students must be invited to participate in their own IEP meetings whenever transition services are discussed. This requirement emphasizes the importance of student voice and agency in the transition process, recognizing that students are best positioned to articulate their own hopes, dreams, and support needs. Active participation empowers students to take ownership of their futures, fostering skills like self-advocacy and decision-making that are crucial for adult life (Wehmeyer et al., 2012).

Despite the strength of IDEA's language, implementation continues to vary across districts and states. Some transition plans fulfill the letter of the law without genuinely engaging students in meaningful preparation for adulthood (Beatson et al., 2023). Realizing the full intent of IDEA requires more than procedural compliance; it demands that educators embrace transition planning as a student-centered, transformative process that prepares young people with disabilities to thrive beyond the classroom.

The IEP's Role in Transition Planning

The IEP functions as the central instrument for delivering high-quality transition services. As mandated by IDEA, the IEP must articulate a coordinated set of activities designed to help students move from school to postsecondary pursuits (IDEA, 2004, § 300.320(b)). Transition planning within the IEP ensures that educational experiences are tailored to each student's unique strengths, needs, preferences, and aspirations. When thoughtfully constructed, the IEP serves as a road map that guides students toward their future goals, weaving together academic learning, vocational preparation, and life skills development.

A critical element of the transition-focused IEP is the development of measurable postsecondary goals. These goals must be rooted in age-appropriate assessments and connected to instructional programming, related services, community experiences, and activities of daily living, where appropriate. They form the backbone of transition planning, linking student interests with actionable plans (Test et al., 2009). Without clearly articulated postsecondary goals, transition services risk becoming fragmented and disconnected from the realities of adult life.

Student participation is a vital aspect of IEP development during transition years. IDEA requires that students be invited to attend IEP meetings where transition planning occurs, placing them in a leadership role in shaping their educational futures (IDEA, 2004, § 300.321(b)). Engaging students actively not only promotes self-determination but also fosters confidence, self-awareness, and resilience. Transition-focused IEPs that meaningfully include students are more likely to reflect their authentic goals and lead to stronger postsecondary outcomes (Wehmeyer et al., 2012).

Despite the legal mandates, challenges remain in making the IEP a truly effective tool for transition. Some IEPs suffer from vague goals, inadequate assessments, or insufficient interagency coordination (Beatson et al., 2023). To maximize the IEP's power in transition planning, educators must move beyond minimal compliance and engage deeply with students and families to create dynamic, individualized plans that prepare students for a full, meaningful adult life.

Key Concepts: Postsecondary Goals and Transition Assessments

Two fundamental concepts underpin effective transition planning under IDEA: measurable postsecondary goals and age-appropriate transition assessments. Measurable postsecondary goals provide the anchor for the transition plan, articulating what the student hopes to achieve after leaving high school in areas such as education, employment, and independent living. These goals must be specific, outcome oriented, and actionable, setting a clear direction for educational and service planning (IDEA, 2004, § 300.320(b)).

Age-appropriate transition assessments are essential tools for developing meaningful postsecondary goals. Assessments may include interest inventories, vocational aptitude tests, functional skill assessments, or interviews with the student and family. These tools help gather critical information about the student's strengths, needs, preferences, and interests. Without these assessments, postsecondary goals risk being generic or disconnected from the student's authentic aspirations (Test et al., 2009).

Effective transition assessments are not one-time events but ongoing processes. As students grow and change during adolescence, repeated assessments allow IEP teams to refine and adjust goals to remain aligned with the student's evolving interests and capacities. High-quality assessments capture not only academic and vocational skills but also critical life skills needed for community engagement and independence (Wehmeyer et al., 2012). When measurable post-secondary goals and transition assessments are implemented with fidelity, they ensure that transition planning is meaningful, individualized, and empowering. As outlined in **Table 2.1**, these elements are foundational to high-quality transition planning and must be approached with intentionality and equity. Conversely, when these elements are weak or absent, students are left without clear pathways to adulthood. Prioritizing robust assessments and goal development is essential to creating transition plans that genuinely prepare students with disabilities for successful postsecondary outcomes (Beatson et al., 2023).

Table 2.1 – Core Components of High-Quality Transition Planning Under IDEA (2004)

Component	Description	Equity Considerations
Measurable Postsecondary Goals	Specific goals based on student interests and preferences in education, employment, and living	Must be culturally and linguistically relevant; reflect student voice and lived experience
Age-Appropriate Transition Assessments	Ongoing assessments used to guide planning and goal setting	Should be accessible, strengths-based, and adapted for students with diverse backgrounds
Coordinated Set of Activities	Interrelated steps, including instruction, services, and community experiences	Requires interagency collaboration and inclusive opportunities across racial/socioeconomic lines
Student Involvement in the IEP Process	Active participation by the student in planning meetings and decisions	Essential for self-determination; often limited for students from underserved communities
Family and Interagency Collaboration	Engagement of families, Vocational Rehabilitation Agencies, colleges, and community organizations	Collaboration must be intentional, multilingual, and inclusive of historically marginalized families

Section 504, ADA, and Postsecondary Access

Beyond IDEA, two other landmark pieces of legislation play vital roles in ensuring access to postsecondary environments for students with disabilities: Section 504 of the Rehabilitation Act of 1973 and the Americans with Disabilities Act (ADA) of 1990. Section 504 prohibits discrimination on the basis of disability in any program or activity receiving federal financial assistance. This includes public schools, colleges, universities, and vocational programs, ensuring that students with disabilities have equal access to educational opportunities (Rehabilitation Act, 1973).

The ADA extends similar protections into the broader public sphere, covering not only educational institutions but also employment, transportation, and public accommodations. Title II of the ADA applies to public entities, including public schools and colleges, while Title III applies to private colleges and universities. Together, Section 504 and the ADA ensure that students with disabilities have the right to reasonable accommodations and equal participation in all aspects of postsecondary life (ADA, 1990).

Transition planning must incorporate an understanding of these laws to prepare students for the realities of postsecondary education and employment. Unlike in K-12 settings, postsecondary institutions do not have the same obligations to modify curricula or fundamentally alter programs; instead, they are required to provide reasonable accommodations to ensure equal access. Helping students understand their rights under Section 504 and the ADA, and equipping them to advocate for accommodations, is a critical component of transition education (Madaus, 2011).

Effective transition plans bridge the gap between the entitlement-based services of K-12 education and the civil-rights-based supports available in adulthood. Students who are knowledgeable about Section 504 and the ADA are better positioned to access needed supports, persist in postsecondary environments, and navigate the challenges of independent living and employment. Preparing students with this legal knowledge empowers them to self-advocate and succeed in diverse postsecondary settings.

Core Components of Effective Transition Planning

High-quality transition planning is built upon a foundation of essential practices that empower students with disabilities to navigate their futures with confidence and success. These practices move beyond mere legal compliance, centering the strengths, aspirations, and voices of students as the driving force behind their transition journeys. In this section, I examine five critical components of effective transition planning: student-centered planning, family involvement, interagency collaboration, career and technical education (CTE) combined with work-based learning, and the development of self-determination skills. Together, these components form an integrated approach to preparing students not only for graduation but for full participation in postsecondary education, employment, and community life. By investing in these core areas, educators and stakeholders can create transition systems that are truly transformative rather than transactional.

Student-Centered Planning

Student-centered planning is a foundational principle of effective transition services, ensuring that students with disabilities are active participants in setting goals and identifying the supports they need. Rather than making assumptions about a student's future, educators must create structures that prioritize the student's voice in all aspects of transition planning. This approach aligns with the mandates of IDEA (2004), which require that students be invited to their IEP meetings when transition services are being discussed. Students' insights into their interests, strengths, and aspirations are critical to developing meaningful postsecondary goals and service plans.

Active student participation fosters ownership of the transition process and promotes critical life skills such as self-advocacy, decision-making, and goal-setting. Research shows that when students are engaged as leaders in their own transition planning, they are more likely to achieve positive outcomes in education, employment, and independent living (Test et al., 2009). Encouraging students to express their goals, ask questions, and weigh options strengthens their ability to navigate adult systems of support and advocate for themselves in postsecondary settings.

Implementing student-centered planning requires a deliberate shift in how educators facilitate IEP meetings and transition conversations. Instead of dictating options to students, professionals must listen actively, offer flexible pathways, and build plans that genuinely reflect each student's individual vision for adulthood. Tools such as person-centered planning models and student-led IEPs offer practical strategies for increasing student engagement in meaningful ways (Wehmeyer et al., 2012).

Despite its clear benefits, barriers to student-centered planning persist. Time constraints, lack of educator training, and entrenched adult-driven decision-making models can limit authentic student participation (Beatson et al., 2023). Overcoming these challenges demands a commitment to cultural change within schools, emphasizing student agency as not only a best practice but also a right. In doing so, transition planning becomes a powerful tool for empowerment rather than compliance.

Family Involvement

Families play a critical role in the transition planning process, serving as advocates, decision-makers, and vital sources of support for students with disabilities. Family members possess unique knowledge of the student's history, strengths, needs, and dreams, making their involvement essential to developing effective transition plans (Test et al., 2009). IDEA (2004) requires that families be invited to participate in IEP meetings, recognizing the importance of collaboration between home and school to support successful transitions.

Family engagement in transition planning contributes to stronger student outcomes across education, employment, and community participation. Research consistently demonstrates that students whose families are actively involved in planning are more likely to experience successful postsecondary transitions (Aleman-Tovar & Burke, 2022). Families help students set realistic and ambitious goals, navigate service systems, and advocate for accommodations and supports necessary for adult life.

Effective family involvement goes beyond inviting parents to meetings; it involves establishing genuine partnerships characterized by mutual respect, shared decision-making, and open communication. Schools must provide families with the information, resources, and cultural responsiveness needed to meaningfully engage them in the transition process (Morningstar et al., 2017). Tailored supports are especially important for culturally and linguistically diverse families, who may face additional barriers to participation.

Challenges such as limited understanding of transition rights, logistical constraints, or negative past experiences with schools can hinder family involvement. To address these challenges, educators must prioritize family-friendly practices, flexible scheduling, translation services, and proactive relationship-building. Empowering families strengthens the transition planning process and ensures that students have the robust network of support they need to succeed beyond high school.

Interagency Collaboration

Interagency collaboration is a cornerstone of effective transition planning, ensuring that students with disabilities receive coordinated support across education, employment, and community living domains. IDEA (2004) emphasizes the importance of involving representatives from agencies likely to provide or pay for transition services in the IEP process (§ 300.321(b)). Collaboration between schools, vocational rehabilitation agencies, higher education institutions, and community organizations can bridge the often-fragmented systems students must navigate after leaving high school.

Successful interagency collaboration fosters seamless transitions, connecting students to postsecondary education programs, employment supports, independent living services, and healthcare systems. Research highlights that when schools partner effectively with outside agencies, students are more likely to achieve competitive employment and pursue postsecondary education (Beatson et al., 2023). Early and sustained collaboration helps students and families build trust in adult systems, easing the anxiety that often accompanies major life transitions.

Key strategies for strengthening interagency collaboration include developing formal agreements (such as memoranda of understanding), sharing information across systems with appropriate consent, and holding joint planning meetings with students and families present. Transition coordinators can serve as critical liaisons, ensuring that agencies work together rather than in isolation. Collaboration is most successful when it is built on shared accountability and a common commitment to student-centered outcomes.

Despite its promise, interagency collaboration can be challenging due to bureaucratic barriers, funding silos, and differing eligibility criteria across systems. Educators must proactively address these challenges by building relationships with agency partners early, advocating for systemic reforms, and centering the needs and goals of students and families above organizational limitations. True collaboration reflects a collective responsibility for preparing students with disabilities for adulthood.

Career and Technical Education and Work-Based Learning

CTE and work-based learning opportunities are critical components of effective transition planning for students with disabilities. CTE programs offer students hands-on experiences, technical skills training, and industry-recognized certifications that can lead to meaningful employment after graduation. Integrating real-world learning into the high school experience prepares students for the realities of the labor market and broadens their postsecondary options (Morningstar et al., 2017).

Work-based learning experiences, such as internships, job shadowing, apprenticeships, and paid employment, are especially powerful tools for transition success. Research consistently shows that students with disabilities who participate in early work experiences are more likely to secure competitive employment as adults (Test et al., 2009). Work experiences help students build critical skills such as communication, time management, teamwork, and problem-solving, while also fostering independence and self-confidence.

Embedding CTE and work-based learning into the transition process requires intentional planning. Educators must collaborate with employers, community organizations, and workforce development agencies to create accessible and supportive opportunities for students. Adaptations and accommodations may be necessary to ensure full participation, and ongoing job coaching or mentoring can further enhance students' success in work environments (Wehman et al., 2015).

Barriers to access remain a concern, particularly for students with significant disabilities or those from marginalized backgrounds. Schools must actively work to dismantle these barriers by advocating for inclusive CTE programs, providing transportation support, and ensuring equitable access to meaningful work experiences. Preparing students through real-world learning is not merely an enhancement to education, it is an essential foundation for adult independence and fulfillment.

Building Self-Determination Skills

Developing self-determination skills is fundamental to preparing students with disabilities for successful transitions to adulthood. Self-determination encompasses a range of capacities, including decision-making, goal-setting, problem-solving, and self-advocacy (Wehmeyer et al., 2012). Students who are self-determined are more likely to achieve their postsecondary goals, maintain employment, pursue higher education, and live independently.

Self-determination must be explicitly taught and nurtured throughout a student's educational experience. Strategies include involving students in setting their own IEP goals, teaching self-advocacy in classroom settings, offering opportunities for choice-making, and encouraging students to reflect on their strengths and interests. Curricula such as the Self-Determined Learning Model of Instruction (SDLMI) provide research-based frameworks for building these essential skills within school environments (Wehmeyer et al., 2012).

Promoting self-determination also requires shifting adult attitudes about student autonomy. Too often, students with disabilities are shielded from making decisions or assuming responsibility for their own lives, reinforcing dependency rather than fostering independence. Educators and families must recognize that supporting self-determination sometimes involves allowing students to experience natural consequences, learn from mistakes, and develop resilience.

Systemic barriers, such as low expectations, restrictive service models, or lack of training, can inhibit the development of self-determination skills. Overcoming these barriers involves creating inclusive educational cultures that view every student as capable of leading their own lives. Transition planning rooted in self-determination is not only more effective but also more just, honoring the dignity and potential of students with disabilities as they prepare to navigate their futures.

Challenges and Barriers in High School Transition Planning

Despite decades of legislation and research affirming the importance of transition planning, too many students with disabilities still encounter systems that fail to prepare them for adulthood. These failures are not isolated oversights but the result of deeply entrenched structural barriers that reproduce inequity and limit opportunity. Transition planning often becomes a bureaucratic exercise rather than a transformative process, especially for students who have been historically marginalized. In this section, I examine five critical challenges undermining effective transition planning: the prioritization of compliance over quality; enduring equity gaps based on race, class, and language; the pervasive impact of low expectations and ableism; chronic resource shortages; and wide variation in services across states and districts. Addressing these barriers is not merely about improving practices, it is about dismantling systems of oppression and reimagining transition planning as a tool for justice, liberation, and genuine opportunity for all students with disabilities.

Compliance Versus Quality

While transition planning is legally mandated under IDEA (2004), too often schools treat it as a compliance exercise rather than a meaningful, student-centered process. In many cases, transition planning is reduced to checking boxes on a form to satisfy audit requirements, with little regard for whether the services outlined genuinely reflect students' aspirations and support their postsecondary success. This approach strips transition planning of its transformative potential, relegating it to a bureaucratic task rather than an empowering educational practice (Beatson et al., 2023).

When compliance takes precedence over quality, students are left with transition plans that are generic, vague, and disconnected from their real goals. Postsecondary objectives may be written in broad terms without individualized supports, transition assessments may be superficial or outdated, and students themselves may be minimally involved in the process. Such plans fail to prepare students for the complexities of adult life, undermining the very purpose of transition services (Test et al., 2009).

High-quality transition planning, by contrast, is dynamic, individualized, and responsive. It demands that schools invest time in developing authentic relationships with students and families, conduct meaningful assessments, and coordinate real-world experiences aligned with student interests. Moving beyond compliance requires a shift in both mindset and practice, centering the transition process on empowerment rather than procedural requirements (Wehmeyer et al., 2012).

Addressing the gap between compliance and quality calls for systemic change, including robust professional development for educators, stronger accountability measures tied to outcomes rather than paperwork, and the elevation of student voice as the core driver of planning. Only when transition services are treated as fundamental to student success will they realize their full potential to transform lives.

Equity Gaps

Significant equity gaps persist in transition planning and outcomes for students with disabilities, particularly among students of color, students from low-income backgrounds, and English learners. Research shows that these students are less likely to receive high-quality transition services, participate in rigorous academic and career preparation, or achieve positive postsecondary outcomes than their white, more affluent peers (Aleman-Tovar & Burke, 2022). These disparities reflect broader systemic inequities in education and must be directly addressed to create just transition systems.

Students from marginalized communities often face multiple layers of discrimination that intersect with disability status. Lower expectations from educators, limited access to resources, and language barriers can all contribute to inequitable transition planning experiences. For example, English learners with disabilities may struggle to receive transition assessments and services in their preferred language, undermining the authenticity of their postsecondary goals (Morningstar et al., 2017). Without intentional, culturally responsive practices, transition planning risks reinforcing patterns of exclusion and marginalization.

Efforts to close equity gaps must begin with recognizing and confronting the structural barriers that students face. This includes providing bilingual transition services, offering culturally relevant career exploration opportunities, involving families from diverse backgrounds in meaningful ways, and ensuring that transition goals reflect students' cultural values and community contexts (Aleman-Tovar & Burke, 2022). Transition planning must be rooted in a commitment to equity, not simply equality, tailoring supports to meet the unique needs of each student.

Ultimately, addressing equity gaps is not only a moral imperative but also essential for fulfilling the promise of transition services. When systems invest in culturally sustaining and socially just transition practices, they empower all students to envision futures rich with opportunity, dignity, and choice.

Low Expectations and Ableism

Low expectations and ableist attitudes among educators, counselors, and other professionals pose significant barriers to effective transition planning for students with disabilities. Ableism, the systemic privileging of nondisabled ways of thinking and being, often manifests in the transition process through assumptions that students with disabilities are incapable of achieving higher education, competitive employment, or independent living (Annamma et al., 2013). These biases can drastically limit the range of opportunities presented to students and undermine their self-confidence.

Research consistently shows that expectations matter. Students whose educators hold high expectations for their future success are more likely to pursue and achieve ambitious postsecondary goals (Beatson et al., 2023). Conversely, when transition planning is constrained by low expectations, students are often tracked into segregated settings, sheltered workshops, or narrow employment pathways, regardless of their actual interests and abilities. Such practices not only violate students' rights but also diminish their potential.

Counteracting low expectations and ableism requires a deliberate commitment to fostering a strengths-based perspective on disability. Educators must recognize that disability is a natural part of human diversity and that students with disabilities possess a wide range of talents, interests, and aspirations. Transition plans must be built around these assets, challenging deficit-based thinking and opening doors to inclusive, high-quality postsecondary options (Wehmeyer et al., 2012).

Professional development that addresses implicit bias, cultural competency, and disability justice principles is critical to transforming mindsets. Empowering students with disabilities to lead their own transition planning, and ensuring that their goals are met with high expectations and strong supports, is essential for creating truly inclusive and equitable futures.

Resource Constraints

Resource constraints remain a formidable obstacle to effective transition planning in many schools and districts. Limited staffing, insufficient funding, lack of specialized training, and weak community partnerships often mean that even well-intentioned educators struggle to provide the depth and quality of transition services that students deserve (Morningstar et al., 2017). Without adequate resources, transition planning can become rushed, superficial, or entirely overlooked.

Many schools lack dedicated transition coordinators, forcing general education or special education teachers, already burdened with heavy caseloads, to manage complex transition processes with little support. Staff may also lack access to up-to-date training on best practices, legal mandates, or culturally responsive approaches to transition planning (Beatson et al., 2023). The absence of strong partnerships with vocational rehabilitation agencies, postsecondary institutions, and community-based organizations further isolates schools and limits the breadth of services available to students.

Addressing resource constraints requires systemic investment. Schools must prioritize funding for transition coordinators, professional development, and interagency collaboration infrastructure.

Creative partnerships with local businesses, nonprofits, and higher education institutions can expand opportunities without placing additional financial strain on school budgets. Advocacy at the state and federal levels is also essential to ensure that transition services receive the funding and policy support they require.

Ultimately, building robust transition systems demands that schools recognize transition planning as an essential, not optional, component of education for students with disabilities. Only by investing time, expertise, and resources can schools fulfill their responsibility to prepare students for meaningful postsecondary lives.

Variation Across States and Districts

The quality of transition planning varies significantly across states and districts, creating a patchwork system in which students' access to effective services often depends on geography rather than need. Although IDEA (2004) establishes federal mandates for transition services, the interpretation and implementation of these requirements are left largely to states and local education agencies. As a result, students in different communities experience vastly different levels of support and opportunity.

In some states and districts, transition planning is robust, beginning early, involving multiple stakeholders, and focusing on student-centered outcomes. In others, transition services are minimal, narrowly focused on compliance, or initiated too late to be meaningful (Beatson et al., 2023). Factors contributing to this variation include differences in state policies, funding mechanisms, training standards, and political priorities. Students in under-resourced or rural areas often face additional barriers due to limited community services and employment opportunities.

This inconsistency has profound implications for educational equity. Students who happen to live in a district with strong transition programs have greater chances of achieving postsecondary success, while others are left at a disadvantage through no fault of their own. Such disparities highlight the need for national standards, greater oversight, and more consistent accountability measures to ensure that every student receives high-quality transition planning regardless of location (Test et al., 2009).

Addressing variation across states and districts requires both top-down and grassroots efforts. State departments of education must provide clearer guidance and stronger monitoring, while local educators and advocates must push for resources, reforms, and practices that center student empowerment and opportunity. Building a more consistent and equitable transition system is essential for honoring the promise of IDEA and advancing justice for all students with disabilities.

Starting Early

Best Practices for High-Quality Transition Planning

In the face of persistent systemic barriers, adopting high-quality transition practices is not just a matter of educational improvement, it is a matter of justice. Students with disabilities deserve transition planning that honors their full humanity, recognizes their diverse strengths, and positions them as leaders in shaping their own futures. Transition services must move beyond compliance checklists and token gestures, embracing practices that actively dismantle ableism and expand opportunity. In this section, I highlight six best practices essential for creating transformative transition experiences: starting planning early, adopting strengths-based approaches, embracing culturally responsive frameworks, using authentic assessments, embedding transition learning throughout daily instruction, and centering student voice. These practices, grounded in research and justice, offer a vision of transition planning that prepares students not merely to survive but to thrive in postsecondary life.

Starting Early in Transition Planning

Effective transition planning begins well before students approach graduation. Initiating conversations about future goals in middle school, rather than waiting until later high school years, provides students with more time to explore options, build skills, and make informed decisions about their futures. IDEA (2004) mandates that transition planning be included in the IEP no later than age 16, but best practices suggest starting even earlier, ideally by age 14 or younger (Test et al., 2009).

Starting early allows students to engage in meaningful career exploration activities, develop academic and vocational skills over time, and participate in community experiences that broaden their understanding of adult life. Early transition planning also enables educators to scaffold instruction in ways that progressively build toward postsecondary readiness, rather than attempting to compress all preparation into the final years of high school (Beatson et al., 2023).

Moreover, involving students in early planning fosters a sense of ownership and agency in their educational journeys. As students reflect on their interests and aspirations, they can set more intentional academic and career goals, increasing their motivation and engagement. Families also benefit from early transition conversations, gaining time to understand available options, advocate for needed supports, and plan for the future alongside their children (Morningstar et al., 2017).

Delaying transition planning until late high school years limits students' opportunities to make adjustments, participate in experiential learning, or build the skills necessary for independence. Early, proactive planning is a critical foundation for successful postsecondary outcomes, transforming transition services from a last-minute checklist into a meaningful, developmental process.

Strengths-Based Approaches

Transition planning that focuses on student strengths rather than deficits is essential for empowering students with disabilities to envision successful futures. Traditional special education practices have often emphasized remediation and deficit correction, but a strengths-based approach shifts the narrative to highlight talents, interests, and capabilities (Wehmeyer et al., 2012). This perspective affirms that all students, regardless of disability label, possess valuable skills and potential to contribute to their communities.

A strengths-based approach begins by identifying what students do well, academically, socially, creatively, or vocationally, and then building transition plans that leverage those assets. For example, a student who demonstrates strong interpersonal skills might explore careers in counseling, customer service, or community organizing.

By aligning transition goals with personal strengths, educators help students develop realistic, motivating pathways to adulthood.

Research indicates that strengths-based transition planning increases student engagement, self-confidence, and persistence in postsecondary settings (Test et al., 2009). It fosters positive identity development by allowing students to see themselves as capable contributors, rather than viewing their disabilities as limitations to overcome. This shift has powerful implications for academic achievement, career attainment, and social inclusion.

Implementing strengths-based approaches requires educators to adopt asset-oriented mindsets, utilize positive assessment tools, and engage in collaborative conversations with students and families. Transition plans rooted in strengths promote dignity, respect, and hope—core elements of a truly inclusive and empowering educational experience.

Culturally Responsive Transition Planning

Culturally responsive transition planning acknowledges that students' identities, including race, ethnicity, language, and disability, shape their experiences, aspirations, and opportunities. Ignoring these dimensions risks creating transition plans that are disconnected from students' realities and community contexts (Aleman-Tovar & Burke, 2022). A culturally responsive approach intentionally centers students' cultural assets and lived experiences in the planning process.

Effective culturally responsive planning involves building authentic relationships with students and families, understanding their values and expectations for adulthood, and honoring diverse ways of knowing, working, and contributing. Transition goals must be relevant not only to students' individual strengths but also to their cultural identities and community realities (Morningstar et al., 2017). For example, career aspirations may reflect communal values or involve entrepreneurship that draws on cultural traditions.

Culturally responsive transition planning also addresses systemic inequities that disproportionately affect students from marginalized communities. Educators must confront their own biases, advocate for equitable access to opportunities, and design supports that are linguistically and culturally appropriate. Providing bilingual services, recognizing the role of extended family in decision-making, and connecting students to culturally affirming mentors are all strategies that enhance culturally responsive practice.

When transition planning is culturally responsive, it validates students' full identities and expands their possibilities for future success. By rejecting one-size-fits-all models, educators can create transition pathways that are not only individualized but also deeply affirming, helping students navigate postsecondary life with a strong sense of belonging and purpose.

Using Authentic Assessments

Authentic assessments play a critical role in developing meaningful transition plans that truly reflect students' interests, strengths, and goals. Traditional assessments often focus narrowly on academic skills, but authentic transition assessments capture a broader and more personalized range of competencies, including work skills, communication abilities, life skills, and self-determination (Beatson et al., 2023).

Authentic assessments are typically student-driven and may include structured interviews, career interest inventories, community-based observations, vocational aptitude tests, and portfolios of student work. These tools allow students to demonstrate their skills in real-world or simulated settings, providing richer and more actionable information than standardized tests alone (Test et al., 2009).

Using authentic assessments empowers students to engage in self-reflection and goal setting. It also ensures that transition plans are tailored to students' genuine interests and capacities rather than assumptions made by adults. Repeated authentic assessments over time allow IEP teams to track growth, adjust goals, and respond to evolving aspirations, making the transition process dynamic and responsive.

Educators must be intentional in selecting assessments that are culturally appropriate, accessible, and aligned with students' communication styles and needs. Authentic assessments shift the focus from what students "lack" to what they can do, helping to frame transition planning as a pathway to empowerment rather than remediation.

Embedding Transition in Everyday Instruction

Transition planning should not occur in isolation from the broader educational experience; instead, it must be embedded into everyday instruction across academic and vocational settings. When transition skills, such as goal setting, problem-solving, self-advocacy, and career exploration, are woven into daily lessons, students have more opportunities to develop these competencies naturally and meaningfully (Morningstar et al., 2017).

Embedding transition across instruction means that general education and special education teachers alike integrate future planning into their curricula. For example, a math class might include financial literacy lessons related to budgeting for independent living, while an English class might involve writing career interest essays or practicing job interview skills. This integration ensures that transition learning is relevant, contextualized, and sustained throughout the school day.

Research shows that when transition skills are taught as part of academic content rather than as add-on activities, students are better prepared for postsecondary expectations (Test et al., 2009). Embedding transition into instruction also normalizes conversations about adulthood, making them a regular and expected part of students' educational journeys rather than something reserved for special meetings or final years.

To successfully embed transition skills, schools must provide professional development, curricular resources, and administrative support to teachers. Collaboration among special educators, general educators, career counselors, and community partners enhances the coherence and impact of this approach, leading to more seamless and effective preparation for life after high school.

Empowering Student Voice

Empowering student voice in the transition planning process is essential for creating plans that are truly meaningful and individualized. Transition planning must center the dreams, preferences, and self-advocacy of students, positioning them as leaders in shaping their futures rather than passive recipients of services (Wehmeyer et al., 2012).

Student-led IEP meetings are a powerful strategy for empowering voice. In these meetings, students present their goals, lead discussions about their strengths and support needs, and collaborate with the team to design services that align with their aspirations. This practice builds critical self-determination skills and fosters a sense of agency that will serve students well in postsecondary education, employment, and community life (Test et al., 2009).

Creating opportunities for student voice requires more than inviting students to attend meetings; it involves intentionally preparing them to participate, valuing their contributions, and creating spaces where they feel respected and heard. Schools must provide instruction in self-advocacy, offer coaching and practice opportunities, and ensure that transition planning processes are accessible and student-friendly (Beatson et al., 2023).

When student voice is authentically empowered, transition planning becomes a transformative process that honors students' identities, respects their autonomy, and builds the skills they need to navigate adulthood with confidence and purpose.

References

Aleman-Tovar, J., & Burke, M. (2022). A review of the literature about transition planning experiences among culturally and linguistically diverse families of youth with disabilities in the United States. *International Review of Research in Developmental Disabilities, 63,* 51–102.

Annamma, S. A., Connor, D. J., & Ferri, B. A. (2013). Dis/ability critical race studies (DisCrit): Theorizing at the intersections of race and dis/ability. *Race Ethnicity and Education, 16*(1), 1–31. https://doi.org/10.1080/13613324.2012.730511

Americans with Disabilities Act of 1990, 42 U.S.C. § 12101 et seq.

Beatson, R., Quach, J., Canterford, L., Farrow, P., Bagnall, C., Hockey, P., ... & Mundy, L. K. (2023). Improving primary to secondary school transitions: A systematic review of school-based interventions to prepare and support student social-emotional and educational outcomes. *Educational Research Review,* 40, 100553.

Individuals with Disabilities Education Act of 2004, 20 U.S.C. § 1400 et seq.

Madaus, J. W. (2011). The history of disability services in higher education. *New Directions for Higher Education, 154,* 5–15. https://doi.org/10.1002/he.429

Morningstar, M. E., Lombardi, A., Fowler, C. H., & Test, D. W. (2017). A college and career readiness framework for secondary students with disabilities. *Career Development and Transition for Exceptional Individuals, 40*(2), 79–91. https://

doi.org/10.1177/2165143415589926

Rehabilitation Act of 1973, 29 U.S.C. § 701 et seq.

Test, D. W., Fowler, C. H., Richter, S. M., White, J., Mazzotti, V., Walker, A. R., & Kortering, L. (2009). Evidence-based practices in secondary transition. *Career Development for Exceptional Individuals, 32*(2), 115–128. https://doi.org/10.1177/0885728809336859

Wehman, P., Sima, A., Ketchum, J., West, M., Chan, F., & Luecking, R. (2015). Predictors of successful transition from school to employment for youth with disabilities. *Journal of Occupational Rehabilitation, 25*(1), 323–334. https://doi.org/10.1007/s10926-017-9710-4

Wehmeyer, M. L., Shogren, K. A., Palmer, S. B., Williams-Diehm, K., Little, T. D., & Boulton, A. (2012). The impact of the Self-Determined Learning Model of Instruction on student self-determination. *Exceptional Children, 86*(1), 92–109. https://doi.org/10.1177/0014402919856749

CHAPTER 3

The Intersection of Disability, Race, and Socioeconomic Status

Intersectionality Defined

Intersectionality, a term introduced by Kimberlé Crenshaw (2022), describes how multiple social identities, such as race, gender, class, and disability, interact to create unique experiences of oppression and marginalization. Rather than viewing these identities as separate, Crenshaw emphasized that they interlock and compound, meaning that the discrimination faced by someone at these intersections cannot be fully understood by examining each identity in isolation. Intersectionality offers a framework for analyzing how systems of power overlap and operate simultaneously.

In the context of education, intersectionality provides a necessary lens for understanding why certain students are disproportionately underserved. A Black student with a disability may face racism and ableism simultaneously, neither of which can be disentangled from the other. Their challenges in school are not the sum of two separate discriminations, but rather a complex and integrated experience of exclusion. Intersectionality calls educators to move beyond siloed approaches to identity and toward a more holistic understanding of how inequity operates.

This framework also challenges dominant educational practices that often default to a one-size-fits-all model of support. School systems frequently respond to disability, race, and poverty with narrowly targeted interventions that fail to recognize the ways these identities intersect. For example, a program designed to support students with disabilities may not account for racial biases in behavioral referrals, or a diversity initiative may ignore issues of accessibility altogether.

Intersectionality further reveals how institutional policies, though often neutral on the surface, can produce inequitable outcomes when they fail to address the specific realities of multiply marginalized students. This includes special education placement processes, discipline policies, and even transition planning procedures that overlook how systemic forces shape students' experiences in schools.

Ultimately, defining intersectionality is about naming the structures of power that organize schooling. It invites educators, researchers, and policymakers to ask not just who is being underserved, but why, and to design educational systems that recognize the full humanity of every student.

Relevance to Schools

Intersectionality is deeply relevant to education because schools serve as one of the most visible sites where overlapping inequalities converge. Although educators may not intend to perpetuate discrimination, school policies, curricula, and practices often reflect broader societal hierarchies that marginalize students at the intersections of disability, race, and socioeconomic status. Ignoring these intersections allows systems to uphold inequity while appearing neutral or even supportive.

For instance, students of color with disabilities are more likely to be placed in self-contained special education classrooms, suspended at higher rates, and excluded from gifted or college preparatory programs (Annamma et al., 2013). These disparities are not coincidental; they reflect the cumulative effects of racism, ableism, and classism in the structure and delivery of educational services. Intersectionality helps us understand how these outcomes are not simply about individual bias, but are deeply embedded in institutional practice.

By applying an intersectional lens, educators can better analyze why some students are disproportionately identified for special education services, why certain families are less likely to attend Individualized Education Program (IEP) meetings, and why transition plans often fail to reflect students' aspirations. Intersectionality makes clear that without a systemic understanding of power and identity, interventions will fall short.

Intersectionality empowers educators to move away from deficit-based models and toward more inclusive, asset-oriented approaches. Instead of asking what students "lack," intersectional frameworks encourage schools to ask how institutional barriers can be removed and how systems can adapt to meet students where they are. This shift is foundational to any equity-oriented practice.

Finally, recognizing intersectionality is a commitment to justice. It means acknowledging that students are not blank slates or isolated data points; they are full beings shaped by history, culture, family, community, and identity. Education that fails to recognize this complexity will inevitably fail the students it aims to serve.

Chapter Road Map

This chapter explores how disability, race, and socioeconomic status intersect in the lives of students, particularly as they navigate K-12 schools and prepare for postsecondary transition. It begins with a historical overview of how educational systems have pathologized and segregated students with disabilities and students of color, laying the foundation for today's inequities. This history is essential for understanding current disproportionality in special education, discipline, and postsecondary access.

The next section addresses data and research that document how students at these intersections are disproportionately funneled into restrictive educational settings, often denied access to rigorous academic content, and subjected to higher rates of disciplinary action. These patterns are explored not only as outcomes of policy failures, but as reflections of systemic power and implicit bias. Special attention is given to how transition planning often reproduces these inequalities through lowered expectations and limited postsecondary pathways.

From there, the chapter centers the voices of students, families, and educators whose lived experiences bring nuance to these issues. These narratives offer insight into the daily realities of navigating intersecting oppressions in schools. Through these stories, the chapter highlights both the harm of current practices and the resilience of those who resist them.

The final two sections focus on actionable change. First, a set of best practices is offered, grounded in research and guided by intersectional principles. These include culturally responsive pedagogy, the use of authentic assessments, collaborative transition planning, and policy advocacy. The second offers a call to action for school leaders, practitioners, and policymakers to reimagine transition planning not as a bureaucratic requirement, but as a vehicle for social justice.

By mapping these themes, this chapter provides a framework for readers to critically examine the ways in which educational systems are structured, and how they can be restructured, to support the thriving of students living at the intersection of disability, race, and poverty.

Disability Perceptions Over Time

The perception of disability in educational systems has evolved significantly over the past century, yet remnants of past beliefs still shape the experiences of students today. Early in the 20th century, disability was often viewed through a medical or deficit-based lens, with students labeled as "feebleminded," "crippled," or "uneducable" (Ryan et al., 2022). These labels justified the exclusion of disabled children from public schools and reinforced the idea that disability was a personal tragedy to be managed rather than a social identity to be respected.

Institutionalization and segregation were the dominant approaches to disability for much of the 1900s. Many children with physical, intellectual, or emotional disabilities were placed in separate institutions or "special" schools, isolated from their nondisabled peers. Educational systems mirrored broader societal beliefs that people with disabilities should be hidden away or corrected, not included in mainstream environments. This approach devalued disabled lives and denied students access to the academic and social development available in general education settings.

In the post–World War II era, advocacy by parents and disability rights organizations began to challenge these exclusionary practices. Grassroots movements pushed for the recognition of the educational rights of children with disabilities, demanding that they be given the same opportunities as their peers. This advocacy laid the groundwork for legal challenges and, eventually, legislative reforms that reshaped how disability was viewed in schools.

Despite these gains, vestiges of the medical model remain. Many schools continue to focus on "fixing" students with disabilities through remediation and compliance with procedural mandates rather than fostering inclusive environments that affirm disability as part of human diversity. This enduring focus on deficits can marginalize students and limit their full participation in school life. When disability is seen as separate from other identities, such as race or class, the complexity of students' experiences is overlooked.

Understanding this historical evolution is essential for educators and policymakers who seek to build inclusive systems. Recognizing how past beliefs continue to influence present-day practices allows us to more clearly identify and dismantle barriers. The shift from exclusion to inclusion must be accompanied by a shift in mindset, from viewing disability as a limitation to embracing it as a source of identity, pride, and community.

Racial and Economic Disparities

The history of education in the United States is deeply rooted in systemic racism and economic exclusion. From legally segregated schools to funding models based on local property taxes, educational access and opportunity have long been stratified by race and class. For students of color, particularly Black, Latinx, and Indigenous students, the promise of public education has often been undermined by policies designed to maintain racial hierarchies and economic inequality (Ladson-Billings, 2006).

The landmark case *Brown v. Board of Education* (1954) declared racial segregation in public schools unconstitutional, but its promise of integration has never been fully realized. In many urban districts, schools remain segregated by race and class due to residential segregation, unequal school funding, and biased disciplinary practices. Students in under-resourced schools frequently attend buildings in disrepair, have less access to experienced teachers, and face overcrowded classrooms, all of which impact learning outcomes.

Economic disparities further compound educational inequities. Families living in poverty often face challenges such as food insecurity, unstable housing, and limited access to healthcare, all of which affect students' academic engagement and school success. For students with disabilities in these communities, the barriers are even more pronounced. Underfunded schools may lack the personnel, training, or materials to implement high-quality special education services, resulting in inadequate support for students who need it most.

These historical patterns of exclusion have created enduring structural inequities. Students of color from low-income backgrounds are disproportionately placed in special education, often under subjective categories like emotional disturbance or intellectual disability (Harry & Klinger, 2014). This overrepresentation is not simply a matter of misidentification but reflects the influence of cultural bias, deficit thinking, and systemic neglect.

To move toward educational equity, it is critical to confront this historical legacy honestly. Racial and economic disparities are not accidental, they are the product of policy decisions, institutional inertia, and a failure to prioritize justice. Addressing them requires not only more equitable funding and inclusive practices but also a fundamental reimagining of how schools view and support all learners, particularly those at the intersection of race, class, and disability.

Legislative Milestones

The history of disability rights in education is marked by a series of legislative victories that have expanded access and opportunity for students with disabilities. The first major breakthrough came with the Rehabilitation Act of 1973, particularly Section 504, which prohibited discrimination based on disability in programs receiving federal funding. This law was foundational in shifting the conversation from charity to civil rights, recognizing that students with disabilities were entitled to the same educational access as their peers.

Building on this momentum, Congress passed the Education for All Handicapped Children Act in 1975, later renamed the Individuals with Disabilities Education Act (IDEA). This law mandated that students with disabilities receive a Free Appropriate Public Education (FAPE) in the Least Restrictive Environment (LRE). It also introduced the requirement for IEPs, designed to ensure that students receive tailored supports based on their unique needs (Yell, 2018).

IDEA was a landmark shift. It not only guaranteed access to public education for millions of children who had previously been excluded, but also created accountability structures for how schools served these students. It emphasized procedural safeguards, parental involvement, and the use of nondiscriminatory evaluations. Over time, IDEA has evolved through several reauthorizations to include stronger transition planning mandates, the promotion of inclusive practices, and increased focus on outcomes.

Despite these advances, implementation of IDEA has often fallen short of its ideals. Many districts struggle with underfunding, over-reliance on compliance checklists, and persistent inequities in service delivery. The spirit of inclusion is frequently overshadowed by deficit-based frameworks that emphasize limitations rather than potential. These gaps between law and practice disproportionately affect students of color and those from low-income backgrounds.

Understanding legislative milestones is vital not only to celebrate progress but also to recognize the ongoing work required to ensure full access and equity. Laws like IDEA and Section 504 provide powerful tools, but without sustained advocacy, community engagement, and culturally responsive implementation, their transformative potential remains unrealized. The future of equitable education depends on honoring both the legal victories of the past and the lived realities of students today.

Overrepresentation of Minority Students

Disproportionality in Special Education

One of the most persistent and troubling patterns in American education is the disproportionate representation of students of color and students from low-income backgrounds in special education programs. Although special education was designed to provide tailored supports for students with disabilities, it has often served as a site where systemic inequities are reproduced rather than disrupted. Disproportionality is not a random occurrence; it is the result of historical, structural, and interpersonal forces that shape how disability is defined, perceived, and acted upon within schools. In this section, I examine three key contributors to disproportionality: the overrepresentation of minority students, the impact of socioeconomic factors, and the pervasive influence of systemic biases. Understanding these dynamics is essential for reimagining special education as a tool for equity rather than exclusion.

Racialized Patterns in Special Education

A persistent concern in special education is the overrepresentation of students of color, particularly Black, Latinx, and Indigenous students, in special education programs. Research has consistently demonstrated that these students are more likely to be identified as having disabilities compared to their white peers, especially in subjective categories such as emotional disturbance and intellectual disability (Skiba et al., 2011). This pattern raises serious questions about whether identification practices reflect actual need or systemic bias embedded within educational institutions.

The overrepresentation of minority students in special education cannot be fully explained by differences in disability prevalence. Instead, it reflects broader issues of inequality in early childhood experiences, healthcare access, school readiness, and classroom instruction. When students of color enter under-resourced schools that lack culturally responsive pedagogy or positive behavioral supports, they are more likely to be perceived as needing special education services, even when their challenges are primarily environmental.

Placement patterns are also a significant issue. Students of color identified with disabilities are more likely to be placed in more restrictive environments, separated from general education peers, and excluded from college preparatory curricula (Annamma et al., 2013). These placements have lasting effects, limiting access to rigorous academic content, reducing expectations, and ultimately constraining postsecondary opportunities.

Overrepresentation intersects with discipline disparities. Black students with disabilities, for example, face disproportionately high rates of suspension, expulsion, and referral to alternative education settings. The combination of special education identification and exclusionary discipline compounds disadvantage and criminalizes disability and racial identity simultaneously.

Addressing overrepresentation requires systemic changes in evaluation practices, educator preparation, school climate, and accountability measures. It demands that schools not only identify disability accurately but also interrogate the broader structures that lead students of color to be disproportionately labeled and segregated under the guise of support.

Socioeconomic Factors

Socioeconomic status is a critical factor influencing the identification of students with disabilities. Students from low-income backgrounds are more likely to be referred for special education evaluation, often based on challenges rooted in environmental deprivation rather than intrinsic disabilities (Morgan et al., 2017). Factors such as exposure to poverty-related stress, limited early childhood education, inadequate healthcare, and unstable housing can all contribute to academic struggles that are sometimes misinterpreted as evidence of disability.

Children living in poverty often have less access to high-quality preschool programs, which can affect language development, social skills, and early literacy. When these students enter elementary school, their lack of exposure to structured educational environments can be mistaken for developmental delays or learning disabilities. Educators may view these differences through a deficit lens rather than considering the structural inequities that shape school readiness.

Access to comprehensive healthcare is another critical variable. Students from low-income families are less likely to receive early diagnoses or interventions for conditions such as ADHD, speech impairments, or developmental disabilities. As a result, when difficulties emerge in school, they may be identified later and through less nuanced evaluations, increasing the likelihood of misclassification and placement in special education programs (Harry & Klinger, 2014).

The pressures facing schools serving high-poverty populations can exacerbate these issues. Overburdened teachers, limited access to intervention services, and accountability demands tied to standardized test scores can create incentives to refer struggling students for special education services as a way of accessing additional supports or reducing academic pressure.

Recognizing the role of socioeconomic factors in disability identification calls for a shift toward equity-driven evaluation practices. Schools must differentiate between true disabilities and educational impacts of poverty, ensuring that students receive the appropriate academic, social, and emotional supports without being unnecessarily labeled or segregated.

Systemic Biases

Systemic biases in education are deeply intertwined with patterns of disproportionality in special education. Implicit biases, unconscious attitudes or stereotypes that affect understanding, actions, and decisions, play a significant role in how educators interpret student behavior and academic performance (Skiba et al., 2011). These biases often operate without malicious intent, yet their effects are profound, leading to disproportionate referrals, evaluations, and placements for students of color. As illustrated in Figure 3.1, these intersecting forces—ableism, racism, and poverty—compound educational barriers and help explain the persistent patterns of overrepresentation in special education programs.

Bias can influence every stage of the special education process. For example, teachers may be more likely to interpret the behaviors of Black or Latinx students as defiant or oppositional, rather than as expressions of frustration, trauma, or cultural communication styles. These interpretations can trigger special education referrals under categories like emotional disturbance, often without adequate consideration of alternative explanations.

Systemic structures, such as biased assessment tools, Eurocentric curriculum standards, and exclusionary discipline policies, further entrench disproportionality. Standardized tests and evaluation measures often reflect dominant cultural norms, disadvantaging students whose experiences and knowledge do not align with these assumptions (Annamma et al., 2013). The very criteria used to identify disability may therefore be culturally loaded and inequitable.

School systems often lack the training and capacity to engage in culturally responsive evaluation practices. Without intentional efforts to confront bias and restructure evaluation and placement systems, disproportionality will persist. Efforts to "fix" individual students without addressing institutional bias are destined to fall short.

Challenging systemic bias requires a multifaceted approach. Schools must invest in ongoing professional development focused on culturally responsive pedagogy, antiracist practices, and critical reflection on disability and difference. Only by transforming the beliefs, practices, and policies that shape education can we create systems where all students are accurately supported and equitably served.

Figure 3.1 – Intersecting Barriers Affecting Postsecondary Transition

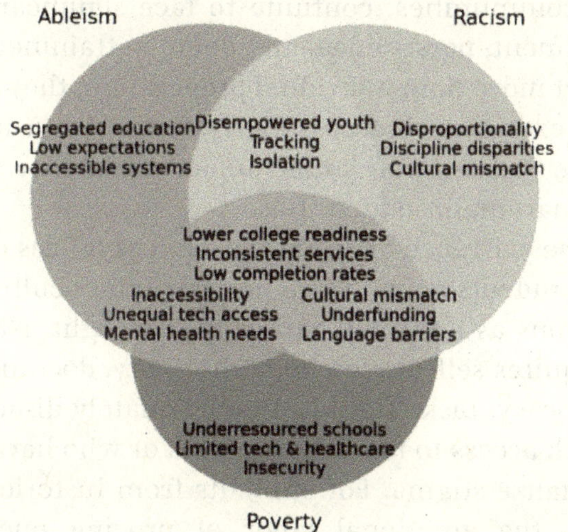

Unequal Academic Outcomes

Life After Exit: Compounding Inequities Beyond School

The inequities that shape students' K-12 experiences do not end at high school graduation; they extend deeply into adulthood, compounding over time to limit access to postsecondary education, meaningful employment, independent living, and holistic well-being. For students with disabilities who are also racialized and economically marginalized, the transition out of school often marks not a gateway to opportunity, but an intensification of systemic exclusion. Postsecondary institutions, job markets, and healthcare systems remain ill equipped to accommodate or affirm their complex identities, resulting in persistent gaps in outcomes. This section examines how the intersection of disability, race, and socioeconomic status continues to shape life trajectories after school, particularly in the areas of higher education, employment, and health, revealing that educational injustice does not stop at the schoolhouse door, but reverberates throughout the life course.

Barriers to Higher Education

Access to higher education remains one of the clearest indicators of long-term economic and social mobility, yet students with disabilities, particularly those who are Black, Latinx, Indigenous, or from low-income communities, continue to face significant barriers to college enrollment, persistence, and degree attainment. These disparities reflect more than individual preparation; they are the result of structural exclusion, inaccessible systems, and a higher education landscape that remains largely unaccountable to students with intersecting marginalized identities.

Despite the existence of disability services offices on most campuses, many students encounter a postsecondary culture that views accommodations as a burden rather than a right. Navigating college often requires self-disclosure of disability, documentation, and repeated advocacy, tasks that disproportionately disadvantage students who lack access to formal diagnoses or who have been socialized to internalize stigma. For students from historically excluded communities, the emotional labor of proving one's legitimacy becomes a barrier in and of itself.

Furthermore, the narrow pathways carved out for students with disabilities in K–12 settings often do not prepare them for the academic and social demands of higher education. Those who were placed in restrictive classrooms or denied rigorous coursework may arrive at college with fewer credits, limited academic confidence, and little exposure to self-directed learning. When these gaps are not met with institutional support, they are framed as personal failures rather than the predictable outcomes of systemic inequity.

Intersectional experiences of racism, ableism, and classism only compound these challenges. Students of color with disabilities often find themselves navigating campuses where they are hyper-visible in some ways and completely invisible in others, rarely represented in leadership roles, academic curricula, or campus-wide conversations about equity. As a result, many drop out before completing a degree, often burdened by debt and disillusionment with a system that promised inclusion but delivered marginalization.

Creating truly inclusive postsecondary institutions requires more than ADA compliance or isolated support programs. It calls for structural reform: inclusive pedagogy, universal design for learning, culturally responsive disability services, and accountability metrics that center equity. Without these systemic changes, higher education will continue to function as a gatekeeper rather than a liberator for multiply marginalized students with disabilities.

Exclusion From Economic Opportunity

The promise of education is often tied to employment and economic self-sufficiency, but for students with disabilities who are also racialized and economically marginalized, the labor market replicates the same patterns of exclusion they faced in school. Unemployment and underemployment rates remain disproportionately high for these individuals, and the types of jobs available to them are often segregated, low-paying, and lacking in advancement opportunities. The transition from school to work is not simply difficult; it is systematically obstructed.

Vocational rehabilitation services, when available, are too often underfunded, narrowly targeted, or difficult to navigate. Many young adults with disabilities are funneled into sheltered workshops or low-wage service jobs, regardless of their interests, skills, or potential. These placements reflect lowered expectations and a failure of systems to invest in meaningful employment pathways, especially for youth of color who have already been pushed to the margins of opportunity.

Students from low-income families often lack the social capital and professional networks that facilitate access to internships, mentorships, or competitive employment. Those with disabilities face additional obstacles related to workplace discrimination, lack of reasonable accommodations, and transportation barriers. These structural conditions, not individual ambition, explain the stark gaps in employment outcomes across race, class, and disability lines.

The economic exclusion of disabled people of color is not incidental, it is embedded in hiring practices, workplace norms, and policy design. Antidiscrimination laws such as the Americans with Disabilities Act (ADA) offer some protection, but enforcement remains inconsistent, and too many workplaces operate without a genuine commitment to equity. Employment support systems that fail to account for intersectionality end up serving the most privileged within the disability community, leaving others behind.

Transforming this reality requires coordinated action: inclusive workforce development programs, enforcement of antidiscrimination laws, public investment in accessible transportation and housing, and corporate accountability for equitable hiring and retention. Employment should not be a privilege accessible only to a few; it is a right tied to dignity, agency, and economic justice.

Health, Disability, and Structural Neglect

Health outcomes for individuals with disabilities are shaped not only by biology but by the social and institutional conditions in which they live. Students with disabilities who are also from racially and economically marginalized communities face significant disparities in access to physical and mental healthcare, both during their school years and into adulthood. These disparities are the direct result of structural neglect, systemic racism, and ableism in the healthcare system.

Mental health support is a critical area of concern. Youth who have experienced educational exclusion, repeated discipline, and limited opportunities are more likely to report anxiety, depression, and trauma-related symptoms. Yet access to culturally competent, disability-affirming mental health services is often limited, especially in communities already facing provider shortages and inadequate insurance coverage. The result is a mental health crisis that remains largely unacknowledged and unaddressed.

Physical health outcomes also reflect systemic failures. Individuals with disabilities are more likely to face chronic conditions, but preventive care is often inaccessible due to transportation challenges, provider bias, or lack of accessible facilities. Students who age out of school-based services often experience a steep drop in health support, with few adult systems in place to ensure continuity of care. These gaps are especially dangerous for those without economic means or social support networks.

Healthcare systems often mirror the same bureaucratic hurdles and surveillance that students with disabilities have experienced in schools. Navigating benefits, qualifying for services, and advocating for basic accommodations can be exhausting and retraumatizing, particularly for people of color who must also contend with racial bias and historical medical mistrust. The burden of navigating these systems is unjustly placed on individuals rather than addressed through policy change.

A truly equitable vision of transition must include access to comprehensive, culturally responsive, and affirming healthcare. This includes not only physical and mental health services, but also reproductive care, gender-affirming treatment, and support for neurodivergent and chronically ill individuals. Health justice is disability justice, and both must be central to any serious conversation about postsecondary transition.

Voices From the Margins: Case Studies and Personal Narratives

Statistics and policy analyses are critical tools for understanding systemic inequities, but they can never fully capture the human experiences that lie behind the numbers. To truly reckon with the impact of intersecting oppressions in education, we must center the voices of students, families, and educators navigating these realities every day. Their narratives offer insight into how systems of racism, ableism, and economic injustice shape not just schooling, but aspirations, identities, and futures. In this section, I share composite case studies and personal reflections that illuminate the lived consequences, and the enduring resilience, of those at the intersection of disability, race, and poverty.

Student Story: Navigating Barriers to Belonging

Jamal, a Black high school student diagnosed with a learning disability, spent much of his educational career in segregated classrooms. From elementary school onward, he was consistently placed in remedial courses, often removed from general education settings under the justification that he "needed more structure." Despite expressing early interest in becoming an engineer, Jamal was steered away from advanced math classes by counselors who believed the coursework would be "too challenging." His potential was diminished not by ability, but by the systemic failure to nurture it.

Throughout high school, Jamal struggled with internalized ableism and racialized stereotypes about intelligence. He rarely saw teachers who looked like him or who affirmed his aspirations. In IEP meetings, his presence was often perfunctory, and decisions were made without his meaningful input. College was discussed as a distant possibility rather than an expectation.

Still, Jamal persisted. A mentorship program with Black engineers at a local community organization shifted his sense of possibility. Through this experience, he learned about historically Black colleges and universities (HBCUs) and the support systems available there. With community support and self-advocacy training, Jamal successfully enrolled in a pre-engineering program after graduation.

Jamal's story is not an exception; it is a reflection of how resilience emerges in spite of, not because of, educational structures. His journey reminds us that supporting marginalized students requires more than access; it demands active, intentional affirmation of their dreams, their dignity, and their rightful place in spaces of power.

Family Story: Fighting for Dignity and Access

The Martinez family, recent immigrants from El Salvador, faced multiple barriers when seeking special education services for their daughter, Sofia, who was diagnosed with autism. Language barriers, cultural stigma around disability, and unfamiliarity with the American school system created significant hurdles. At IEP meetings, translation services were inconsistent, and critical documents were often only available in English, limiting the family's ability to fully engage in decision-making.

Educators frequently framed Sofia's challenges through a deficit lens, suggesting placement in a segregated life skills classroom with minimal academic instruction. When Mrs. Martinez questioned whether more inclusive settings were available, she was met with subtle discouragement and warnings about Sofia "falling behind." The message was clear: Sofia's future should be one of containment, not possibility.

Refusing to accept this narrative, the Martinez family sought out advocacy organizations that provided bilingual support and education on disability rights. Empowered with information, they successfully advocated for Sofia's placement in a general education classroom with appropriate supports. Though the road was not without obstacles, Sofia began to thrive academically and socially when provided with access to inclusive environments.

The Martinez family's experience highlights how systemic barriers often silence immigrant families and families of color in special education processes. Their advocacy underscores the need for culturally responsive practices, true language access, and a fundamental shift from deficit-thinking to strength-based engagement with families.

Educator Reflection: Confronting Systemic Complicity

Mr. Johnson, a special education teacher working in a predominantly low-income urban school, described his growing discomfort with the ways students of color with disabilities were treated within his school. Over time, he noticed patterns: Black boys were disproportionately placed in emotional disturbance categories, Latina students with language differences were mislabeled with intellectual disabilities, and students' strengths were rarely discussed in IEP meetings.

Initially, Mr. Johnson felt trapped within the system, believing that his role was limited to compliance with district mandates. But after participating in antiracist and disability justice professional development, he began to see how his silence and procedural focus perpetuated harm. He realized that neutrality in an unjust system is complicity.

Mr. Johnson shifted his practice by centering student voice, challenging deficit language in IEPs, and advocating for inclusive placements. He began collaborating with general education teachers to ensure his students had access to rigorous content and extracurricular opportunities. He also worked to build stronger relationships with families, recognizing that advocacy must be collective and community driven.

His journey was not without pushback. He faced resistance from administrators and colleagues uncomfortable with disrupting the status quo. Yet he persisted, understanding that small acts of resistance, when sustained and collective, can catalyze systemic change.

Mr. Johnson's reflection underscores a critical truth: Educators must move beyond performative allyship and engage in active disruption of the policies and practices that marginalize students. Change is possible, but it requires courage, humility, and an unwavering commitment to justice.

The experiences of students like Jamal, families like the Martinezes, and educators like Mr. Johnson make clear that systemic injustice is not theoretical; it is lived daily in schools, meetings, classrooms, and policy decisions. Their stories reveal not only the profound harm caused by ableism, racism, and economic exclusion, but also the possibilities for resilience, resistance, and transformation when individuals and communities refuse to accept marginalization as inevitable. However, storytelling alone is not enough. To move from understanding to action, we must translate these lived realities into tangible reforms. In the next section, I outline best practices and policy recommendations that center justice, disrupt systems of oppression, and reimagine transition planning as a tool for equity and liberation.

Best Practices and Policy Recommendations

Justice in transition planning will not be achieved through isolated acts of goodwill or minor procedural adjustments. It requires a comprehensive reimagining of how educational systems define success, provide support, and distribute opportunity. In this section, I present a series of best practices and policy recommendations grounded in the lived experiences of marginalized students and families. Each practice is framed not as an optional enhancement, but as a necessary intervention to dismantle systemic inequities and foster authentic belonging and opportunity for students at the intersections of disability, race, and poverty.

Centering Student Voice in All Planning

True justice in transition planning begins with the recognition that students are the primary experts on their own lives. Student voice must be treated not as symbolic or tokenistic, but as the foundation upon which all transition goals, services, and decisions are built. Students should lead their IEP meetings, set their own postsecondary goals, and participate fully in identifying the supports they need to thrive.

Centering student voice requires educators to shift power dynamics, allowing young people, especially those from marginalized backgrounds, to envision futures beyond the narrow expectations often imposed upon them. This includes teaching self-advocacy, providing access to culturally affirming mentors, and embedding student-led reflection and goal-setting into daily instruction, not just annual meetings. Honoring student voice means listening across differences in communication style, culture, and disability. Schools must create multiple, accessible pathways for students to express their goals and concerns, whether through speech, writing, art, or assistive technologies. Student voice must never be contingent on ableist standards of communication or "professionalism."

When students drive their own transition planning, they are more likely to persist through obstacles, resist internalized oppression, and see themselves as agents of change. Transition planning that excludes or diminishes student voice is, by definition, unjust. Institutions must formalize the centrality of student voice through policy, requiring evidence of authentic student leadership in IEP development, transition assessments, and postsecondary goal setting. Justice demands that we trust students to imagine and build futures beyond the limitations imposed upon them.

Implementing Culturally Responsive Transition Planning

Transition planning must affirm the full cultural identities of students and families. Culturally responsive transition planning recognizes that disability does not exist in a vacuum, it is lived alongside race, language, class, gender, and community context. Plans that ignore these intersections risk replicating the very systems of exclusion they are meant to dismantle.

A culturally responsive approach begins with relationship building. Educators must take time to learn about students' families, communities, and aspirations beyond dominant white, middle-class frameworks of success. Postsecondary goals should be aligned not only with individual interests but also with students' cultural values and visions of collective thriving.

Language access is fundamental to culturally responsive practice. Schools must provide all transition-related information in families' home languages, ensure the availability of interpreters at meetings, and recognize that professional jargon often alienates rather than empowers. Authentic communication, not compliance, should be the goal. Culturally responsive transition planning also challenges deficit narratives about students and communities. Instead of framing goals around escaping poverty or dysfunction, plans should celebrate community wealth, cultural resilience, and interdependence as sources of strength. For example, a student aspiring to work in family businesses, mutual aid networks, or community advocacy should be supported just as vigorously as those pursuing 4-year college pathways.

To that end, culturally responsive transition planning must be institutionalized, not left to individual educators' discretion. Districts should be held accountable for training staff in antiracist, culturally sustaining practices and for tracking equity metrics across race, language, and disability status in transition outcomes.

Embedding Transition Skills in Everyday Learning

Preparing students for life after school cannot be relegated to isolated programs or end-of-year activities. Transition skills, such as self-advocacy, problem-solving, career exploration, financial literacy, and independent living competencies, must be integrated into everyday instruction across academic, vocational, and social domains. Embedding transition into daily learning ensures that students practice essential life skills over time, rather than cramming them into a narrow "transition services" window. It also affirms that all students, regardless of label or placement, deserve to envision and prepare for vibrant futures. Transition is not a special education issue, it is an educational justice issue for every learner.

General education teachers, special educators, and counselors must collaborate to create interdisciplinary curricula that connect academic standards to real-world application. A math lesson on budgeting, a science project on accessible design, a language arts unit on advocacy narratives—all of these can serve dual purposes of content mastery and transition preparation. Schools must also dismantle ableist assumptions about who should learn which skills. Far too often, students with intellectual disabilities or students of color with disabilities are denied access to rigorous content under the guise of "life skills training." Justice requires that transition education be expansive, aspirational, and tailored to the unique dreams of each student, not their perceived deficits.

Embedding transition into everyday instruction affirms that preparation for adulthood is a right, not a privilege reserved for a few. It demands a restructuring of pedagogy that sees students not as future burdens on the system, but as future leaders, creators, workers, and change-makers.

Expanding Community Partnerships

No single institution can meet the complex and intersectional needs of students with disabilities who also navigate racial and economic oppression. Schools must build deep, sustained partnerships with community organizations, cultural institutions, healthcare providers, workforce agencies, and postsecondary institutions to ensure that transition planning extends beyond the classroom and into the real-world environments students will encounter after graduation.

Community partnerships are especially critical for students from under-resourced neighborhoods, where access to internships, job shadowing, mentorship, and social services may be limited. Through coordinated efforts, schools can bridge the opportunity gap by connecting students to culturally affirming mentors, disability-led organizations, and work-based learning opportunities that reflect their identities and goals (Swayzer, 2025). These partnerships also model interdependence, reminding students and families that success is communal, not individual.

However, many school-community partnerships remain transactional or tokenistic, limited to one-time events, narrow referral pipelines, or symbolic gestures. A justice-centered approach requires that partnerships be rooted in trust, reciprocity, and shared power. Community organizations should be treated not as add-ons to the education system but as co-educators and co-designers of transition services. Their lived expertise, especially from BIPOC-led and disability justice movements, must be valued alongside academic credentials.

With this in mind, schools must remove barriers that prevent students and families from accessing these partnerships. This includes providing transportation, multilingual outreach, and flexible scheduling for working families. It also means compensating community partners for their labor and acknowledging that access without inclusion is not equity. Expanding and deepening community partnerships moves transition planning from institutional silos to a collective ecosystem of care, learning, and opportunity. It recognizes that justice cannot be achieved within the boundaries of the school alone; it must be built in collaboration with the communities students call home.

Holding Systems Accountable for Equity

To realize justice in transition planning, we must move beyond individual advocacy and toward systemic accountability. Disproportionality, inequitable outcomes, and exclusionary practices are not random; they are measurable, predictable, and preventable. Therefore, schools, districts, and states must be held publicly and transparently accountable for ensuring that transition services advance, rather than undermine, equity for students with disabilities from historically marginalized backgrounds. Accountability must not be an afterthought or a technical add-on; it must be embedded into the very fabric of educational systems as a moral and legal obligation.

Policy must begin with disaggregated, publicly available data. State and district education agencies should be required to report postsecondary outcomes, including college enrollment, competitive employment, and independent living, by race, disability category, language background, gender, and socioeconomic status. These data must be disaggregated annually, not only to satisfy reporting requirements under IDEA and the Every Student Succeeds Act (ESSA), but to equip families, advocates, and local communities with the information needed to press for justice. Transparency exposes patterns and empowers action.

Policymakers should redefine accountability metrics beyond procedural compliance. States must develop equity-centered transition quality indicators that assess the alignment of postsecondary goals to student interests, the cultural responsiveness of transition services, and the degree of authentic student and family engagement. These indicators must be used to inform technical assistance, resource distribution, and program evaluation, not simply compliance audits. Compliance without justice is insufficient, and often, actively harmful.

Systems that perpetuate inequity must face enforceable consequences. State education plans should include mandated equity benchmarks tied to federal funding, and school leaders' performance evaluations should reflect their progress toward dismantling transition-related disparities. Policy should mandate ongoing professional development tied directly to equity outcomes in transition, not generalized training disconnected from practice. Communities must also be granted accessible and enforceable mechanisms to file complaints, demand corrective action, and co-create improvement plans. This is not merely about oversight, it is about redistribution of power.

The path to accountability is not neutral. It requires a conscious commitment to shifting control from systems to the students and families they have historically failed. Justice in transition planning is only possible when schools are accountable not just to bureaucracies, but to the communities they serve, especially those most often silenced. Table 3.1 highlights the intersecting institutional, cultural, and structural barriers that shape the postsecondary experiences of students with disabilities at the margins. Equity must not remain a rhetorical commitment; it must be a measurable, enforceable, and publicly monitored obligation backed by law, policy, and political will.

Table 3.1 – Systemic Forces Shaping Transition Outcomes for Multiply Marginalized Students

Systemic Barrier	Impact on Transition Planning	Equity Implication
Ableism	Leads to lowered expectations, segregated settings, and inaccessible curriculum	Requires universal design, disability-affirming practices, and inclusive pedagogy
Racism	Results in discipline disparities and biased special education referrals	Demands culturally responsive transition assessments and antiracist school culture
Poverty	Limits access to healthcare, tech, and college counseling	Necessitates wraparound supports and intentional outreach to low-income families
Intersectionality	Intensifies barriers when identities overlap	Calls for individualized, justice-centered planning rooted in lived experiences

Conclusion

Throughout this chapter, I have argued that transition planning for students with disabilities cannot be disentangled from the realities of race, class, and systemic oppression. These intersections shape not only access to education, but the very assumptions made about what students can become. We cannot reform special education by tinkering at the margins, we must radically reimagine how we define readiness, success, and inclusion. The case studies, narratives, and data shared here make clear that current systems are failing too many students, not because of a lack of evidence or legal mandates, but because of a refusal to center justice in practice.

A justice-centered vision of transition planning demands early and ongoing engagement, culturally responsive pedagogy, inclusive and rigorous instruction, community-rooted supports, and structural accountability. It requires that we see students as whole people living at complex intersections, not as compliance categories or caseloads. It calls us to dismantle the deficit ideologies and bureaucratic inertia that have long denied students their full educational rights.

But this work is not only about systems, it is about people. It is about the students who continue to dream in classrooms that were never built for them. It is about families who refuse to accept limited futures. And it is about educators, advocates, and leaders who are willing to speak truth to power and build new possibilities from the ground up. The path forward will not be easy, but it is necessary. Our students deserve transition systems that do more than prepare them to survive; they deserve systems that affirm their brilliance, cultivate their agency, and invest in their freedom. Anything less is not justice. It is abandonment.

References

Annamma, S. A., Connor, D. J., & Ferri, B. A. (2013). Dis/ability critical race studies (DisCrit): Theorizing at the intersections of race and dis/ability. *Race Ethnicity and Education, 16*(1), 1–31. https://doi.org/10.1080/13613324.2012.730511

Brown v. Board of Education, 347 U.S. 483 (1954).

Crenshaw, K. (2022). Demarginalizing the intersection of race and sex: A black feminist critique of antidiscrimination doctrine, feminist theory and antiracist politics [1989]. *Contemporary sociological theory, 1*, 354.

Every Student Succeeds Act (ESSA) of 2015, Pub. L. No. 114–95, 129 Stat. 1802.

Harry, B., & Klingner, J. (2014). *Why are so many minority students in special education?: Understanding race and disability in schools*. Teachers College Press.

Individuals with Disabilities Education Act of 2004, 20 U.S.C. § 1400 et seq.

Ladson-Billings, G. (2006). From the achievement gap to the education debt: Understanding achievement in U.S. schools. *Educational Researcher, 35*(7), 3–12. https://doi.org/10.3102/0013189X035007003

Morgan, P.L., Farkas, G., Hillemeier, M.M., & Maczuga, S. (2017). Replicated evidence of racial and ethnic disparities in disability identification in U.S. schools. *Educational Researcher, 46*(6), 305–322. https://doi.org/10.3102/0013189X17726282

Rehabilitation Act of 1973, 29 U.S.C. § 701 et seq.

Ryan, M., Rowan, L., Lunn Brownlee, J., Bourke, T., L'Estrange, L., Walker, S., & Churchward, P. (2022). Teacher education and teaching for diversity: A call to action. *Teaching Education, 33*(2), 194–213.

Skiba, R. J., Horner, R. H., Chung, C. G., Rausch, M. K., May, S. L., & Tobin, T. (2011). Race is not neutral: A national investigation of African American and Latino disproportionality in school discipline. *School Psychology Review, 40*(1), 85–107.

Swayzer, S. (2025). *Developing Individualized Transition Plans (ITPs): Literature Review* (Doctoral dissertation, Alliant International University).

Yell, M. L. (2018). *The law and special education* (5th ed.). Pearson.

PART II

Pathways to Postsecondary Success

CHAPTER 4

College Readiness and Academic Success

The dominant narrative around college readiness often centers on standardized test scores, grade point averages (GPAs), and a narrow set of academic indicators. For students with disabilities, particularly those who are Black, Latinx, Indigenous, low income, or first generation, this framework not only fails to capture their strengths but also obscures the systemic barriers they face in accessing meaningful college preparation. True readiness cannot be measured by data points alone; it must be rooted in opportunity, access, and the removal of obstacles that disproportionately impact multiply marginalized students. This chapter redefines college readiness as a process grounded in equity and justice, not gatekeeping and exclusion.

Students with disabilities have historically been excluded from rigorous academic pathways, often funneled into segregated programs that prioritize compliance over challenge and remediation over rigor. These exclusionary patterns begin early and intensify across grade levels, resulting in underpreparedness that is reflective not of ability, but of restricted opportunity. For students of color with disabilities, these disparities are compounded by racial tracking, discipline disparities, and a lack of cultural responsiveness in the curriculum. As a result, they enter college less likely to have accessed dual enrollment courses, Advanced Placement classes, or guidance counseling tailored to their needs.

College readiness must also include the development of executive functioning skills, academic independence, and knowledge of how to access accommodations. Yet these essential skills are rarely taught explicitly in K-12 settings, especially to students with disabilities. The transition from high school, where support services are often coordinated by adults, to college, where students must self-disclose and advocate, represents a major shift that many are not adequately prepared for. Without targeted instruction in time management, study strategies, and disability self-advocacy, students enter postsecondary education at a structural disadvantage.

Importantly, college readiness must be understood as a culturally mediated process. For students from racially and linguistically diverse backgrounds, "readiness" is often framed in opposition to their lived experiences, cultural ways of knowing, and community-based knowledge systems. Educators must reject one-size-fits-all models and instead center culturally sustaining pedagogy in the transition to higher education. Families, too, must be included as partners in college preparation, especially when navigating systems that are unfamiliar or historically unwelcoming.

This chapter explores the academic, cultural, and structural dimensions of college readiness and academic success for students with disabilities, with an emphasis on intersectionality. It highlights barriers embedded within K-12 systems, offers actionable strategies for preparing students for postsecondary learning environments, and names the institutional reforms required to support their success. If we are to truly support students beyond graduation, we must ensure they are not only academically prepared, but empowered, affirmed, and equipped to navigate and transform the systems ahead.

Foundations of College Readiness

College readiness is often framed through a narrow academic lens, focused on GPAs, standardized test scores, and completion of a prescribed sequence of courses. While these metrics may serve institutional needs, they ignore the systemic barriers that shape students' access to college preparatory opportunities. For students with disabilities, particularly those who are also Black, Latinx, Indigenous, or from low-income communities, such definitions of readiness are exclusionary by design. These students are frequently denied access to the very courses and supports that constitute the foundation of college preparation. Readiness, then, must be reframed as a structural condition, not an individual trait, requiring schools to address opportunity gaps rather than pathologize students (Harry & Klingner, 2014).

Executive functioning skills are among the most important, and overlooked, components of authentic college readiness. Skills such as time management, self-regulation, organization, and persistence are essential for navigating the demands of postsecondary education. Yet these cognitive and behavioral strategies are rarely taught explicitly, particularly in inclusive, culturally responsive ways. Students with disabilities, especially those with learning disabilities or ADHD, may struggle with these areas not due to lack of ability but because they have not been given consistent, strengths-based instruction tailored to their needs (Milford et al., 2021). When these foundational skills are missing, students may be labeled as "unmotivated" or "unprepared," masking the failure of systems to support them.

Equally critical is the quality of academic instruction. Students with disabilities are entitled to access high-level content through pedagogical strategies such as Universal Design for Learning (UDL), scaffolded supports, and differentiated instruction. However, many are instead subjected to rote test preparation, compliance-focused classroom management, and curricula disconnected from their cultural and personal identities. This is especially true for students of color with disabilities, who are often overrepresented in classrooms that emphasize remediation over rigor (Annamma et al., 2013). Such instructional practices reinforce deficit narratives and fail to foster the intellectual curiosity, academic confidence, and critical thinking required for college success.

Access to rigorous coursework is one of the most powerful predictors of college readiness, yet it remains deeply inequitable. Students with disabilities are frequently excluded from Advanced Placement (AP), honors, or dual enrollment programs due to biased gatekeeping, outdated beliefs about ability, or restrictive interpretations of

Individualized Education Programs (IEPs) (Harry & Klingner, 2014). These decisions are often made without student input and reflect institutional norms that equate disability with incapacity. For students of color, these barriers are compounded by racial tracking and limited access to college counseling (Annamma et al., 2013). Denying students access to challenging academic content is not a neutral act, it is a form of systemic exclusion with long-term consequences.

Ultimately, college readiness must be redefined through an equity lens. It is not the responsibility of marginalized students to conform to narrow definitions of preparedness; it is the responsibility of educators and institutions to create conditions in which all students can thrive. This includes reimagining readiness not as a gatekeeping tool, but as an invitation to full participation in academic and social life. Figure 4.1 visually underscores this concept, illustrating how academic, social-emotional, and self-advocacy skills must converge to support postsecondary success. As Mazzotti et al. (2021) argue, meaningful preparation for postsecondary success involves aligning instruction, expectations, and supports with students' strengths, goals, and cultural contexts. Until this becomes the norm, readiness will remain a privilege granted to some rather than a right guaranteed to all.

Figure 4.2 – Intersections of College Readiness Skills for Students with Disabilities

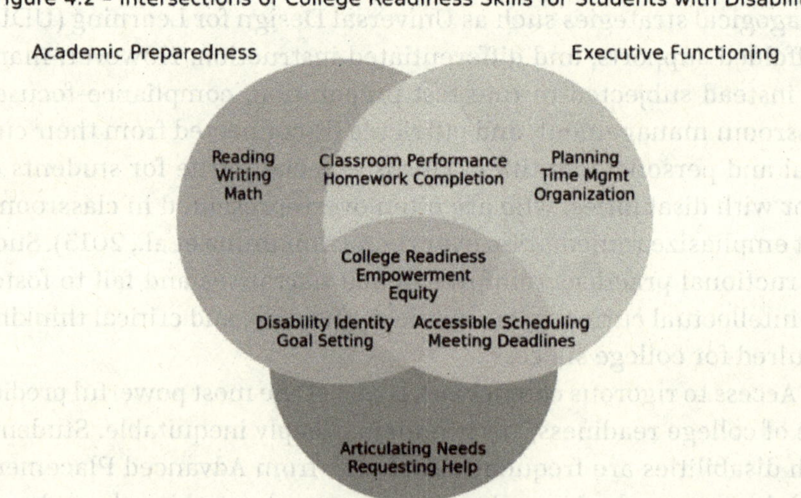

Barriers to Readiness

Despite the legal mandates and growing rhetoric of equity in education, students with disabilities, particularly those from racially and economically marginalized communities, continue to face persistent and predictable barriers to college readiness. These barriers are not simply academic deficits; they are structural outcomes of institutional neglect, ableism, and racism. To move toward justice, we must name and interrogate the forces that limit students' access to rigorous learning, informed guidance, and affirming supports. Table 4.1 provides a critical overview of these barriers and offers asset-based reframing strategies that shift the focus from student deficits to systemic responsibilities. The subsections below highlight five key barriers that obstruct meaningful college preparation: curriculum tracking, low expectations, inadequate guidance, inaccessible college knowledge, and biased assessments.

Table 4.1 – Reframing College Readiness for Students With Disabilities

Traditional/Deficit-Based Approach	**Equity-Based/Justice-Centered Approach**
Emphasizes standardized test scores and GPA	Emphasizes self-advocacy, access, and personalized learning paths
Treats readiness as fixed and individually determined	Treats readiness as relational and shaped by systemic opportunity
Assumes students must adapt to existing systems	Requires institutions to adapt environments to diverse learner needs
Focuses on compliance with academic norms	Focuses on agency, strengths, and holistic skill development
Ignores cultural and disability identities	Affirms intersectional identities and centers lived experience in planning

Curriculum Tracking and Segregated Instruction

One of the most harmful barriers to college readiness is the systematic tracking of students with disabilities into less rigorous and often segregated academic pathways. This process, frequently justified through labels like "life skills" or "functional academics," positions disabled students as incapable of engaging with college-preparatory material. Students of color with disabilities are disproportionately placed in such tracks, reflecting not differences in ability but differences in expectations and opportunity (Harry & Klingner, 2014).

Tracking often begins early and becomes increasingly difficult to escape as students move through secondary school. Once placed in lower-level classes, students have fewer opportunities to take the coursework required for college admissions, including Algebra II, foreign language, and laboratory sciences (Sullivan & Bal, 2013). These course exclusions are rarely questioned and often reinforced by the implicit biases of educators who fail to see the potential in students with intersecting marginalized identities.

This form of academic segregation limits not only content exposure but also peer relationships, teacher expectations, and opportunities to build the study habits and academic stamina needed for postsecondary success. It sends students a powerful message: that their futures are defined by limitations rather than possibilities. Reversing the effects of tracking requires intentional de-tracking policies, inclusive instructional practices, and a radical shift in how schools conceptualize ability.

Low Expectations and Ableist Assumptions

Another insidious barrier to readiness is the culture of low expectations that surrounds students with disabilities, especially those who are Black, Latinx, or from low-income families. Educators and counselors may subtly (or explicitly) discourage these students from pursuing college, steering them instead toward vocational programs or suggesting they "be realistic" about their options (Annamma et al., 2013). These deficit-based messages reflect ableist beliefs that conflate disability with incapacity and compound the effects of racialized assumptions about intellect.

Research has shown that teacher expectations play a critical role in shaping student achievement and persistence (Raley et al., 2021; Rosenthal & Jacobson, 1968). When educators expect less from students, they provide fewer opportunities for challenge, leadership, or support. This becomes a self-fulfilling prophecy, where the system creates the very underpreparedness it later blames on the student.

For students navigating multiple layers of marginalization, low expectations can be internalized as self-doubt. They may come to believe that college is not "for people like them," or that asking for accommodations is a sign of weakness rather than a right. Breaking this cycle requires intentional efforts to build student self-efficacy, normalize disability pride, and affirm college-going identities from early grades onward.

Inadequate College Counseling and Advising

Access to college counseling is a key predictor of postsecondary enrollment, yet students with disabilities, particularly in underfunded schools, often receive minimal or no individualized guidance. School counselors may be overwhelmed by large caseloads or may lack training in disability law, accommodations, or inclusive admissions processes (Trainor et al., 2016). As a result, many students and families are left without the critical information needed to plan for college entry, applications, or financial aid.

Students with disabilities also report that counselors often do not consider them "college bound," and therefore fail to discuss 4-year college pathways, standardized testing timelines, or required coursework. This lack of engagement disproportionately affects first-generation students, multilingual learners, and students of color with disabilities who may not have access to these conversations at home or through community networks.

Effective college counseling must be proactive, culturally responsive, and disability affirming. Counselors must approach every student, regardless of label or test score, as capable of pursuing higher education if given the right supports. Additionally, collaboration between counselors, special educators, and transition coordinators is essential to ensuring students receive holistic and coordinated guidance.

Limited Access to College Knowledge

The term "college knowledge" refers to the set of social and procedural understandings that students need to navigate the transition to higher education, such as how to fill out applications, request accommodations, access support services, and advocate for themselves in a new environment (Conley, 2008). Access to this knowledge is stratified by race, class, and disability, with students from historically excluded communities often having the least exposure.

College knowledge is often transmitted informally, through parents, peers, or extracurricular networks, which means that students whose families have not attended college may be excluded from vital information. For students with disabilities, the challenges are compounded by unclear information about accommodation processes, stigmatizing language, or inconsistent practices across institutions (Meade, 2017). Without early and repeated exposure to college-related knowledge, many students simply do not know what questions to ask or what steps to take.

Schools must not assume students arrive with this knowledge; they must actively teach it. Beginning as early as middle school, educators should integrate college exploration, campus visits, and self-advocacy instruction into the curriculum. This includes helping students understand how disability services work in college, how to request documentation, and how to navigate the transition from the Individuals with Disabilities Education Act (IDEA) to the Americans with Disabilities Act (ADA) and Section 504 protections.

Biased Assessments and Gatekeeping Practices

Standardized testing and other assessment tools often serve as hidden barriers to college readiness for students with disabilities. These assessments frequently reflect dominant cultural norms, privileging certain language styles, cognitive processing patterns, or testing behaviors over others. For students with disabilities who process information differently or require accommodations, traditional assessments can misrepresent their potential (Quenemoen & Thurlow, 2017).

Assessments are often used to determine eligibility for advanced coursework or gifted programs, programs that open doors to scholarships, early college credit, and elite postsecondary opportunities. When assessments are inaccessible or interpreted through biased frameworks, students with disabilities, especially students of color, are disproportionately excluded from these opportunities. This exclusion is rarely questioned, and its impact is cumulative.

Assessment reform must be central to any effort to advance college readiness equity. Schools must adopt multiple measures of student potential and success, ensure that accommodations are available and honored, and invest in culturally and linguistically responsive assessment practices. Most importantly, schools must critically examine how assessments are used: not only what they measure, but how they are interpreted and acted upon.

Transitioning to Academic Independence

Moving from high school to college requires more than academic preparation; it demands a shift in how students manage their learning, advocate for their needs, and navigate systems that offer less structural support. For students with disabilities, this transition is especially challenging. No longer protected by IDEA, they must now rely on the more limited accommodations framework provided by Section 504 and the ADA. The shift from entitlement to eligibility creates steep learning curves that disproportionately affect students from racially and economically marginalized communities (Meade, 2017). In this section, I address the key areas of academic independence that impact college success: disability disclosure, self-advocacy, time and task management, and navigating unfamiliar systems.

Understanding and Navigating Disability Disclosure

Unlike in K-12 settings, where disability accommodations are coordinated by school staff, college students must self-disclose and formally request accommodations through disability services offices. This process requires students to understand their own diagnoses, articulate their needs, and present documentation, skills that many have not been taught (Meade, 2017). For students who have internalized stigma around disability or who come from cultural backgrounds where disability is not openly discussed, this task can be overwhelming.

Disclosure is further complicated by mistrust in institutions, particularly among students of color who have experienced bias or exclusion in K-12 schools. Some students fear that revealing a disability will mark them as less capable or lead to discrimination. Others are unaware of what accommodations exist or how to access them. These gaps in knowledge are not the result of apathy, they are the result of systemic failure to prepare students with the tools and confidence needed to advocate for themselves.

Schools must begin preparing students for disclosure as early as middle school, offering opportunities to practice explaining their learning needs, understand legal differences between IDEA and ADA, and engage in mock college intake sessions. Special education and transition teams should work in tandem with college access programs to ensure students are equipped with both the language and confidence to claim their rights in new environments.

Building Self-Advocacy and Agency

Self-advocacy is a foundational skill for postsecondary success. It includes the ability to understand one's rights, express one's needs, and negotiate for appropriate supports or accommodations. Yet students with disabilities are often socialized into passivity, taught to rely on adults to speak on their behalf or shielded from the decision-making processes of their own education (Raley et al., 2021). For students of color, especially, this disempowerment intersects with cultural messages about respect, authority, and survival in predominantly white institutions.

Educators must explicitly teach self-advocacy skills through culturally responsive pedagogy. This includes engaging students in role-playing scenarios, helping them write scripts for difficult conversations, and modeling how to challenge unjust decisions respectfully but firmly. Students must see self-advocacy not as confrontation but as empowerment, an essential tool for navigating systems that were not designed with them in mind.

Moreover, self-advocacy instruction should be embedded across all content areas, not siloed in special education or counseling services. General educators, too, have a responsibility to foster student voice and agency. When students are invited to lead IEP meetings, select learning strategies, or evaluate their own performance, they begin building the confidence needed to manage academic independence in postsecondary contexts.

Mastering Time, Task, and Workload Management

College places a high premium on self-regulation, time management, and task initiation, skills that many students with disabilities have not been explicitly taught. In high school, daily schedules are fixed, reminders are built in, and staff often monitor task completion closely. In college, students must create their own structure, manage competing priorities, and anticipate long-term deadlines. For students with executive functioning challenges, this shift can lead to academic failure without appropriate preparation (Milford et al., 2021).

Compounding the challenge, students from low-income communities often balance school with work, caregiving responsibilities, or unreliable transportation and housing. These real-life constraints affect focus, attendance, and stamina. Yet postsecondary institutions rarely provide holistic support that acknowledges these intersecting burdens. Instead, the expectation is that all students perform according to a single, middle-class model of academic independence.

Preparing students requires more than study skills workshops. Schools must integrate executive functioning instruction into the core curriculum, with an emphasis on planning, prioritizing, goal setting, and using digital tools to support learning. These supports should be framed as strategies for all learners, not just for those with disabilities, to avoid reinforcing stigma and create a universal culture of success.

Navigating Institutional Systems and Expectations

Understanding the structure of college systems, how to register for classes, communicate with professors, manage financial aid, and use student portals, is another critical aspect of academic independence. These systems are rarely intuitive and often use language or interfaces that assume prior familiarity. Students with disabilities, particularly those without college-going family members, frequently enter college without a map for how these systems operate (Conley, 2008).

What's more, college instructors may lack training in disability inclusion and may resist implementing accommodations, especially in competitive or "weed-out" courses. Students are often left to negotiate conflicts alone, without the advocacy infrastructure provided in high school. Those who lack assertiveness or clarity in their communication may see their accommodations delayed or denied, compromising their academic performance and well-being (Trainor et al., 2016).

High schools must therefore demystify college systems well before graduation. This can include campus visits that go beyond admissions tours, workshops on managing syllabi and email communication, and partnerships with disability services offices to conduct mock intake appointments. Educators must recognize that postsecondary transition is not a leap of faith, it is a process of guided preparation that honors students' right to thrive.

Culturally Responsive College Preparation

College readiness cannot be separated from students' cultural, linguistic, and community identities. For students with disabilities who also identify as Black, Latinx, Indigenous, multilingual, or from low-income families, preparation for postsecondary success must affirm, not erase, their full selves. Too often, college-going frameworks are built around white, middle-class norms that define readiness in ways that exclude the lived realities and assets of marginalized communities. These frameworks treat culture as a barrier rather than a source of strength, and as a result, students are taught to assimilate into college systems rather than reshape them. Culturally responsive preparation shifts this dynamic by centering students' histories, communities, and ways of knowing in both instruction and guidance.

Many students of color with disabilities experience cultural dissonance in school settings long before they begin thinking about college. Curricula often ignore their backgrounds, languages, or family structures, and discipline practices disproportionately punish expressions of cultural identity. These early experiences shape how students view their potential and how they interpret messages about belonging in academic spaces. When college is presented as an environment that requires abandoning or minimizing core aspects of identity, students may disengage before they ever apply. Schools must instead approach college preparation as a process of affirmation, building bridges between students' lived experiences and the expectations of postsecondary institutions (Annamma et al., 2013).

Culturally responsive preparation includes validating students' college aspirations in ways that reflect their communities' values. For some, this might mean attending a local college to stay close to family responsibilities. For others, it may involve choosing institutions with strong cultural or spiritual networks. These decisions should not be interpreted as limitations, but as legitimate expressions of students' goals. Educators must resist deficit perspectives that frame certain pathways as less ambitious and instead support students in pursuing futures that reflect both their ambitions and their responsibilities.

Engaging families is central to this work. Many students with disabilities rely heavily on family support systems, but too often schools communicate college information in ways that are inaccessible or culturally disconnected. Schools must ensure that materials are translated, that meetings are held at times convenient for working families, and that educators build trust through sustained, respectful relationships. Parents and caregivers bring deep knowledge about their children's needs, interests, and values, and must be positioned as partners in the transition process (Harry & Klingner, 2014).

Culturally responsive college preparation is not a one-time intervention or a specialized program. It is a mindset and practice that must be embedded in all aspects of transition planning, from academic counseling and IEP development to classroom instruction and school climate. When students see their identities reflected and affirmed in the messages they receive about college, they are more likely to see higher education as a space where they belong, and one where they can lead. Justice demands that we prepare students not to conform to college, but to shape it in ways that reflect their brilliance and collective histories.

Institutional Responsibility and Systems Change

The responsibility for ensuring college readiness does not rest solely on students or their families, it is a systemic obligation. Far too often, institutions frame readiness as a personal shortcoming rather than recognizing how exclusionary practices, underfunded schools, and inaccessible curricula contribute to disparities in outcomes. While much of the discourse around transition planning focuses on individual student traits, we must shift the lens to interrogate the structures that enable or constrain access. Systems, not students, must be redesigned. In this section, I explore institutional obligations in three domains: inclusive readiness metrics, coordinated support programs, and accountability mechanisms for equity.

Redefining Readiness Through Inclusive Metrics

Current definitions of college readiness rely heavily on standardized assessments, GPA thresholds, and completion of "college prep" course sequences. These metrics reinforce racial, socioeconomic, and disability-based inequities by privileging students who have historically had the greatest access to rigorous coursework and academic support (Conley, 2008). Students with disabilities, especially those in segregated or tracked programs, are often denied the opportunity to even meet these benchmarks, not because of their ability, but because of institutional decisions made on their behalf.

Inclusive metrics must consider multiple measures of readiness, including student voice, demonstrated growth, participation in self-advocacy instruction, and engagement in transition planning. Postsecondary institutions can contribute to this shift by adopting holistic admissions practices that account for context, barriers overcome, and leadership in disability or cultural advocacy. Similarly, high schools must revise how they track "college and career readiness," ensuring that students in special education are not automatically excluded from college-going data reports.

When institutions commit to broader, equity-centered metrics, they not only widen access, they affirm the value of diverse learners and lived experiences. Readiness should not be used to filter out students who don't conform to dominant norms. Instead, it must be reimagined as a commitment to ensure that all students have access to the tools, knowledge, and support they need to thrive.

Investing in Coordinated Transition Support Programs

Students with disabilities transitioning to college require more than individual accommodations, they need institutional ecosystems of support. Programs that integrate academic coaching, disability services, peer mentorship, and family engagement have demonstrated positive impacts on persistence and self-determination (Meade, 2017). However, these programs are not available at most institutions, and where they do exist, they often operate in isolation from broader academic and cultural life.

Public school systems and higher education institutions must establish formal partnerships to ensure continuity of support between high school and college. This includes shared transition liaisons, summer bridge programs tailored for students with IEPs or 504 plans, and guaranteed points of contact at the college level. Partnerships should also extend to disability justice organizations, culturally specific community groups, and family support networks that reflect the identities of the students being served.

Support programs must be rooted in cultural and disability competence. This means hiring staff who understand the intersectional needs of students, designing workshops that address racism, ableism, and classism in college settings, and using data disaggregated by race, disability, and language background to assess program impact. Programs that lack this lens risk reinforcing the same inequities they aim to disrupt.

Ensuring Equity Through Accountability and Policy

Policy must play an active role in ensuring that college readiness initiatives promote, rather than hinder, equity. Too often, education systems report aggregate data that mask disparities and allow inequities to persist unchecked. State departments of education, school districts, and postsecondary institutions must be required to disaggregate college readiness and enrollment data by disability status, race, gender, language background, and income level (U.S. Department of Education, 2016).

Beyond reporting, systems must be held accountable for the outcomes of students with disabilities, not just their participation in programs. Equity benchmarks should be embedded into school improvement plans, and transition-related metrics should be included in state accountability systems under the Every Student Succeeds Act (ESSA). Postsecondary institutions that receive federal funding should be required to demonstrate inclusive practices in admissions, orientation, and academic advising.

Accountability is not about punishment, it is about transparency, responsiveness, and shared responsibility. When institutions are required to examine their practices, address disparities, and engage communities in continuous improvement, real change becomes possible. Equity in college readiness will not come from isolated efforts. It will come from sustained, systemic commitment backed by policy, resources, and the political will to center justice.

Conclusion

Preparing students with disabilities for college success is not simply about academic rigor or exposure to college-level coursework, it is about disrupting the systemic inequities that have long denied these students equitable access to postsecondary opportunities. Throughout this chapter, I have argued that college readiness must be redefined through a lens of justice. This means not only interrogating barriers such as tracking, low expectations, and inaccessible counseling, but also uplifting culturally responsive, student-centered practices that affirm students' full identities. For students who exist at the intersection of disability, race, language, and poverty, preparation must be holistic, affirming, and rooted in the dismantling of ableist and racist educational structures (Artiles, 2013; Ladson-Billings, 2021).

The work of building readiness begins well before high school graduation. It starts with inclusive pedagogy, access to rigorous and relevant curriculum, and intentional instruction in executive functioning, self-advocacy, and college navigation. These foundational skills are not innate, they must be taught explicitly and reinforced across content areas and school years. When schools fail to do this, they are not merely underpreparing students, they are reproducing cycles of exclusion. Students with disabilities must be equipped not only to access college, but to navigate and transform it, using their lived experiences as sources of strength and insight (Sins Invalid, 2016).

Institutions must also be held accountable. The burden of college readiness cannot rest solely on students and families; it must be met with system-wide changes in how readiness is measured, how support is provided, and how success is defined. Postsecondary institutions must shift from compliance to commitment, replacing passive accommodation models with proactive, justice-driven practices that center student voice, honor intersectional identities, and ensure equitable access to every facet of college life (Bensimon, 2004). Similarly, K-12 systems must align resources, metrics, and partnerships with the lived realities of the students they serve.

Policies and funding structures must also reflect this paradigm shift. Federal and state legislation should incentivize inclusive transition programs, support culturally responsive professional development, and require transparent reporting on college outcomes for students with disabilities. Education reform that fails to prioritize equity in transition planning is incomplete. As scholars and advocates have long argued, access without support is not opportunity, it is abandonment (Bell, 1992; Crenshaw, 2013).

As we look toward the next chapter, the focus will turn to the lived experiences of students navigating college systems. Their voices illuminate both the promises and the failures of postsecondary institutions. By centering these stories, we will explore what it truly means not only to arrive at college, but to belong, persist, and thrive. Justice demands more than access; it demands transformation. That transformation begins with us.

References

Annamma, S. A., Connor, D. J., & Ferri, B. A. (2013). Dis/ability critical race studies (DisCrit): Theorizing at the intersections of race and dis/ability. *Race Ethnicity and Education, 16*(1), 1–31. https://doi.org/10.1080/13613324.2012.730511

Artiles, A. J. (2013). Untangling the racialization of disabilities: An intersectionality critique across disability models. *Du Bois Review: Social Science Research on Race, 10*(2), 329–347. https://doi.org/10.1017/S1742058X13000270

Bell, D. (1992). The Performance of Racism. *Sw. UL Rev., 22,* 1103.

Bensimon, E. M. (2004). The diversity scorecard: A learning approach to institutional change. *Change: The Magazine of Higher Learning, 36*(1), 44–52.

Conley, D. T. (2008). *College knowledge: What it really takes for students to succeed and what we can do to get them ready.* John Wiley & Sons.

Crenshaw, K. W. (2013). Mapping the margins: Intersectionality, identity politics, and violence against women of color. In *The public nature of private violence* (pp. 93–118). Routledge.

Harry, B., & Klingner, J. (2014). *Why are so many minority students in special education?: Understanding race and disability in schools.* Teachers College Press.

Ladson-Billings, G. (2021). *Critical race theory in education: A scholar's journey.* Teachers College Press.

Mazzotti, V. L., Rowe, D. A., Kwiatek, S., Voggt, A., Chang, W.H., Fowler, C. H., Poppen, M., Sinclair, J., & Test, D. W. (2021). Secondary transition predictors of postschool success: An update to the research base. *Career Development and Transition for Exceptional Individuals, 44*(1), 47–64. https://doi.org/10.1177/2165143420959793

Meade, S. B. (2017). *Identifying evidence based transition strategies and the barriers to effective transition planning for students with learning disabilities.* Northcentral University.

Milford, T., Lawrence, B., Beamish, W., Davies, M., & Meadows, D. (2021). A strategy for building transition-focused education capacity to support disabled students in Australian schools. *Young Adult Development at the School-to-Work Transition: International Pathways and Processes, 51*(6), 334.

Quenemoen, R. F., & Thurlow, M. L. (2017). Standards-based reform and students with disabilities. In *Handbook of special education* (pp. 203–217). Routledge.

Raley, S. K., Shogren, K. A., Rifenbark, G. G., Lane, K. L., & Pace, J. R. (2021). The impact of the self-determined learning model of instruction on student self-determination in inclusive, secondary classrooms. *Remedial and Special Education, 42*(6), 363–373.

Rosenthal, R., & Jacobson, L. (1968). Pygmalion in the classroom. *The Urban Review, 3*(1), 16–20.

Sins Invalid. (2016). Skin, tooth, and bone: The basis of a movement is our people: A disability justice primer. *Reproductive Health Matters, 25*(50), 149–150.

Sullivan, A. L., & Bal, A. (2013). Disproportionality in special education: Effects of individual and school variables on disability risk. *Exceptional Children, 79*(4), 475–494. https://doi.org/10.1177/001440291307900406

Trainor, A. A., Morningstar, M. E., & Murray, A. (2016). Characteristics of transition planning and services for students with high-incidence disabilities. *Learning Disability Quarterly, 39*(2), 113–124.

U.S. Department of Education, Office of Special Education Programs. (2016). *A transition guide to postsecondary education and employment for students and youth with disabilities.* Washington, DC: Author.

CHAPTER 5

Navigating College Systems With Intersectional Identities

For students with disabilities, entry into postsecondary education is more than a transition, it is a negotiation of belonging within institutions that often marginalize their full identities. While much attention is placed on getting students to college, far less focus is given to what happens once they arrive. Students who navigate the intersecting realities of ableism, racism, linguistic discrimination, and economic hardship often find that college systems are not designed with them in mind. Accommodations may be inconsistent, faculty may be unfamiliar with inclusive pedagogy, and campus culture may silence rather than affirm. This chapter centers the voices and experiences of multiply marginalized college students, those who must work not only to succeed academically, but to survive and thrive in spaces that routinely question their legitimacy. By amplifying their stories and analyzing the structures they navigate, we uncover both the barriers and the strategies that define success beyond access.

Campus Climate and Disability Visibility

The culture of a college campus shapes every aspect of a student's postsecondary experience, from academic engagement to self-advocacy to emotional well-being. Yet for students with disabilities, particularly those who also navigate racial, linguistic, and economic marginalization, campus climate can often feel unwelcoming, inaccessible, and invisibilizing. Despite increased diversity rhetoric in higher education, many institutions remain unprepared to support students with complex, intersecting identities. When disability is acknowledged at all, it is frequently treated as an individual inconvenience rather than a systemic justice issue (Annamma et al., 2013; Harris & Bensimon, 2007). In this section, I examine how campus climate impacts students' sense of belonging and how institutions perpetuate or disrupt disability erasure.

Invisibility by Design: The Absence of Disability in Diversity Agendas

Across many institutions, disability is rarely included in formal diversity, equity, and inclusion (DEI) frameworks. Campus initiatives focused on race, gender, or sexuality often exclude disability entirely, or mention it only superficially. When disability is acknowledged, it is typically framed through a medical or legal lens, an issue of compliance with Section 504 or the Americans with Disabilities Act (ADA), rather than as a critical identity category. This legalistic framing distances disability from broader conversations about systemic injustice and cultural identity, positioning it outside the scope of institutional transformation (Crenshaw, 1997; Jampel, 2018).

The result is a campus culture where disabled students are expected to navigate their needs quietly, without challenging the status quo. Disability services are often tucked away in administrative offices, disconnected from student life, multicultural affairs, or academic support. Students may hesitate to disclose or advocate for accommodations out of fear of being labeled difficult, lazy, or incapable, labels that are compounded when disability intersects with racism, xenophobia, or poverty. This invisibility is not accidental. It is the result of institutional design decisions that treat accessibility as a burden rather than a value and disabled people as afterthoughts rather than stakeholders (Bell, 1992).

Creating visibility requires more than disability awareness campaigns during Disability Heritage Month. It requires embedding disability justice into every aspect of campus life, from curriculum design and faculty training to leadership development and student activism. Institutions must center the voices of disabled students in decision-making spaces and dismantle the cultural norms that define "professionalism," "academic rigor," and "normalcy" in ableist ways (Ladson-Billings, 2021). True inclusion begins when disabled students are no longer asked to choose between receiving support and being seen as legitimate members of the campus community.

The Emotional Tax of Navigating Exclusion

Students with disabilities often carry an invisible emotional burden as they attempt to access systems that were not built for them. This emotional tax is compounded by microaggressions, assumptions of incompetence, and daily experiences of being overlooked, silenced, or questioned. Black and Brown disabled students in particular must navigate the layered reality of managing ableism in spaces already shaped by racial exclusion. The result is a chronic sense of hypervigilance, exhaustion, and self-doubt, conditions that are rarely recognized in academic conversations about "student engagement" or "retention" (Wehmeyer et al., 2012; White et al., 2024).

For many students, the simple act of requesting accommodations can become a fraught experience. Faculty may question the legitimacy of documentation, express frustration over perceived inconvenience, or fail to implement accommodations altogether. These interactions are not isolated incidents, they are manifestations of an institutional culture that prioritizes norms of independence, speed, and performance over equity, access, and care. When students are made to feel like burdens for needing what the law guarantees, the climate becomes not only exclusionary, but psychologically damaging (Artiles, 2013).

Institutions must acknowledge the emotional labor imposed on disabled students and respond by transforming, not merely modifying, campus culture. Faculty and staff must be trained not just in disability compliance, but in disability cultural competency. Mental health services must be attuned to the experiences of students who experience compounded marginalization. And student success metrics must account for the resilience required to persist in environments not designed to support thriving.

Visibility as Resistance: Student Activism and Disability Justice

Despite institutional barriers, disabled students are not passive recipients of policy, they are agents of change. Across the country, students are organizing to challenge ableism on campus, demand accountability from administrators, and reframe disability as a vital part of campus diversity. These movements often draw inspiration from intersectional frameworks and disability justice organizing, pushing beyond access to demand belonging, leadership, and structural change (Jampel, 2018).

Student-led efforts have included campaigns for inclusive restrooms, accessible transportation, sign language interpreters at public events, and the integration of disability studies into general education requirements. These actions are not merely about physical accessibility, they are about reclaiming space and voice in institutions that have historically excluded disabled people from higher education. Importantly, many of these efforts are led by students of color, queer and trans students, and first-generation students who understand that disability justice must be tied to broader movements for racial and economic justice (Annamma et al., 2013).

Institutions have a responsibility to support, not stifle, this activism. This includes providing funding, visibility, and institutional legitimacy to student disability organizations; inviting disabled students to participate in governance structures; and ensuring that accessibility is seen as an institutional value, not an optional accommodation. When campuses shift from seeing disabled students as clients to engaging them as leaders, the climate begins to transform. Visibility is not just about presence, it is about power.

Accessing and Navigating Disability Services in College

While the Individuals with Disabilities Education Act (IDEA) provides robust protections and mandated services in K-12 schools, those rights do not carry over into higher education. Once students graduate from high school, they enter a different legal framework, one governed by Section 504 of the Rehabilitation Act of 1973 and ADA. These laws prohibit discrimination but do not guarantee success, individualized plans, or proactive supports. Students must now advocate for themselves, provide documentation, and navigate an entirely new bureaucratic system. For many, especially those from underrepresented backgrounds, the shift is not just procedural, it is disorienting and unjust.

The Burden of Self-Disclosure and Documentation

In college, students must initiate contact with the disability services office in order to receive accommodations. This process typically requires students to submit documentation, often recent, expensive, and clinically worded, that verifies their disability and specifies functional limitations. For students who had Individualized Education Plans (IEPs) in high school, this shift can be shocking. They may not realize their previous documents are no longer valid, or they may not have access to current evaluations that meet college requirements (White et al., 2024).

Students from low-income backgrounds are particularly vulnerable to documentation barriers. Obtaining updated psychological or medical evaluations can cost hundreds, even thousands, of dollars, placing access to accommodations behind a paywall. Others may be undocumented or uninsured and unable to access any formal diagnosis at all. For students of color, especially Black and Latinx students, these barriers are compounded by prior negative experiences with schooling and healthcare systems, where their needs were misunderstood, ignored, or pathologized (Artiles, 2013; Harry & Klingner, 2006).

Institutions must revise their documentation policies to reduce unnecessary barriers. While upholding the need for appropriate accommodations, colleges can allow provisional or student-provided documentation, accept self-reports during intake, and focus on functional impact rather than medical language. The responsibility should not be on students to prove their worthiness, it should be on institutions to demonstrate their commitment to equity.

A System Built on Compliance, Not Care

Most disability services offices operate from a compliance framework rather than a justice-oriented one. Their primary function is to determine eligibility, assign accommodations, and notify faculty, not to ensure that students are actually supported or thriving. This approach, while legally sound, falls short of what is needed for students to succeed in complex, often exclusionary, academic environments (Harris & Bensimon, 2007). Students may receive extended time or note-taking services but find little support in navigating hostile classrooms, unsupportive faculty, or inaccessible course design.

For students with intersectional identities, the limitations of the compliance model are especially harmful. A Black student with ADHD may receive academic accommodations but still experience racial microaggressions that impact their mental health and academic focus. A first-generation student with autism may be granted sensory-related supports but not be guided through the unwritten norms of campus culture. These gaps reflect a deep mismatch between what students need and what institutions are structured to provide (Jampel, 2018).

Disability services must move toward a holistic, justice-based model. This includes providing wraparound supports, collaborating with mental health services, conducting faculty outreach, and actively engaging in campus equity conversations. When disability offices function as both advocates and educators, not just gatekeepers, students gain access to resources that affirm their full humanity, not just their diagnoses.

Faculty Responsibility and Inconsistency in Implementation

Even when accommodations are approved, their implementation often depends on individual faculty members. Professors may be uninformed, unwilling, or even resistant to modifying their instruction or assessments. Some may question the legitimacy of accommodations, misinterpret disability needs as academic dishonesty, or simply neglect to follow through on institutional guidance. This inconsistency creates unpredictable and inequitable learning environments (Mazzotti et al., 2021; Wehmeyer et al., 2012).

Disabled students report that navigating these dynamics is exhausting and discouraging. Some choose not to use their accommodations out of fear of stigma or retaliation. Others spend significant time and emotional energy chasing down faculty or explaining their needs repeatedly, tasks that subtract from time that could be spent learning. For students already managing racialized or gendered forms of marginalization, these added burdens reinforce a message that they do not belong.

Colleges must mandate disability inclusion training for all faculty, not as a one-time seminar, but as part of ongoing professional development tied to equity and instructional quality. Institutions must also create mechanisms for students to report noncompliance safely and anonymously, with clear follow-up procedures. Accommodations are not favors, they are civil rights.

Building a Culture of Access, Not Exception

Disability services should not be the only place where access is discussed. A truly inclusive campus culture treats access as foundational to pedagogy, design, and community, not as an exception granted to a few. This means faculty designing courses with Universal Design for Learning (UDL) principles, student affairs offices creating sensory-friendly programming, and campus leadership embedding disability into strategic diversity plans (Annamma et al., 2013; Ladson-Billings, 2021).

Disabled students must also see themselves reflected in campus life. This includes the presence of disabled faculty and staff, support groups and cultural programming led by disabled students, and representation in leadership positions. Without this visibility, disability remains marginalized, relegated to a private office visit rather than a public affirmation of identity.

Access is not simply about physical ramps or testing modifications, it is about belonging, power, and transformation. When disability services are reimagined as centers for equity, community-building, and leadership development, they can become catalysts for broader institutional change. Table 5.1 outlines common structural challenges faced by students with disabilities and offers actionable, equity-based strategies institutions can adopt to dismantle those barriers. Until then, students will continue to navigate systems that acknowledge their existence but deny their full participation.

Table 5.1 – Institutional Barriers and Justice-Oriented Responses for Disabled Students With Intersectional Identities

Barrier	Description	Justice-Oriented Response
Invisibility in Diversity Agendas	Disability often excluded from DEI frameworks; addressed only in compliance-based ways	Integrate disability justice into DEI planning, leadership pipelines, and campus life
Burden of Emotional Labor	Students manage microaggressions, disbelief, and institutional neglect	Train faculty in cultural and disability competence; expand mental health supports
Documentation and Disclosure Demands	Costly, clinical documentation required; inaccessible for marginalized students	Accept self-reports, reduce clinical barriers, and prioritize student narratives
Compliance-Driven Disability Services	Services focus on legal minimums, not holistic support	Reframe offices as disability justice hubs with proactive, integrated supports
Faculty Inconsistency and Resistance	Accommodations unevenly implemented; some faculty resist inclusive practices	Mandate faculty training and accountability mechanisms tied to equity
Narrow Definitions of Success	Dominant metrics ignore resilience, community, and cultural values	Broaden definitions of success to include belonging, activism, and interdependence

Belonging, Persistence, and Redefining Success

College success is often narrowly defined through graduation rates, GPAs, and credit accumulation. These metrics, while important, fail to account for the emotional, cultural, and structural realities that shape the experiences of students with disabilities, particularly those who are also navigating racism, linguistic discrimination, or economic hardship. For these students, success cannot be reduced to outcomes alone. It must include a sense of belonging, the ability to thrive on their own terms, and opportunities to lead and contribute within their academic communities. This section explores how persistence is sustained through belonging, how dominant success narratives fail disabled students, and how institutions must rethink what it means to support achievement.

For many disabled students, belonging is the foundation of persistence. Research has consistently shown that students are more likely to stay enrolled and complete their degrees when they feel seen, valued, and included in the social and academic life of their campus (Strayhorn, 2018). Yet campus culture often marginalizes disability, treating it as something to accommodate behind closed doors rather than an identity to affirm publicly. Students who cannot find community, either through formal networks or informal connections, frequently report isolation, disconnection, and questioning their place in college altogether. These experiences are intensified for students who carry multiple marginalized identities, such as students of color, LGBTQ+ students, or first-generation students with disabilities (Jampel, 2018; Ladson-Billings, 2021).

Institutions can cultivate belonging by ensuring that disability is represented in all areas of campus life. This means more than having a disability services office; it means ensuring that disabled students have access to affinity spaces, cultural events, leadership opportunities, and faculty mentorship that affirms their lived experience. It also means recognizing that cultural models of success may differ. Some students may prioritize community engagement, spiritual wellness, or interdependence over individual academic accolades. When institutions embrace a more expansive definition of success, they allow students to define achievement in ways that align with their identities and aspirations (Phillips et al., 2019).

Dominant narratives of college success often reflect white, middle-class, able-bodied norms of productivity, speed, and independence. These ideals marginalize students who need more time, who balance caregiving responsibilities, or who engage in nontraditional paths through higher education. For disabled students, success may include surviving a hostile classroom environment, finding a supportive professor, or learning to self-advocate in ways they were never taught in K-12 schools. These forms of resilience are rarely celebrated in institutional metrics, yet they are profound indicators of growth and persistence (Dolmage, 2017).

Reframing success requires that institutions look beyond numbers and invest in the conditions that allow students to thrive. This includes flexible academic policies, culturally responsive advising, embedded mental health supports, and the recognition of nonacademic contributions such as activism, caregiving, and peer mentorship. As Crenshaw (1991) reminds us, equity is not about treating everyone the same, it is about recognizing and responding to difference. Colleges must ask not only whether students are graduating, but whether they are being respected, supported, and empowered along the way.

Reimagining Disability Support in College

The dominant narrative in higher education celebrates independence as the highest marker of maturity and success. Students are expected to manage their time, self-regulate, advocate for themselves, and complete tasks with minimal support. This framing is deeply embedded in institutional structures, from the language of "self-sufficiency" in student affairs to the emphasis on "personal responsibility" in academic advising. But for many disabled students, particularly those who experience intersectional marginalization, the ideal of independence is not only unrealistic, it is oppressive. It reflects an ableist, white, middle-class norm that disregards cultural values, structural barriers, and the human need for interdependence (Dolmage, 2017; Jampel, 2018).

Disability justice frameworks challenge the primacy of independence by affirming that interdependence is not a weakness, but a vital and relational way of being. The notion that success must be solitary ignores how students rely on community, family, faith, and mutual support systems to survive and thrive. For example, a first-generation student with a learning disability may depend on a peer mentor for time management strategies or emotional encouragement, just as another may rely on family to help navigate confusing institutional paperwork. These support networks are not evidence of failure, they are powerful forms of resistance to exclusionary norms that demand isolation and self-reliance above all else (Garland-Thomson, 2011).

Students of color often bring cultural understandings of collectivism and interdependence into college, but these values are frequently pathologized in academic settings. Asking for help is misread as incompetence. Relying on others is seen as codependency. This misinterpretation erases communal epistemologies and reinforces racialized assumptions about who is prepared for college and who is not. When institutions promote independence without context, they punish students for navigating systems in ways that are culturally adaptive and emotionally sustaining (Ladson-Billings, 2021).

Interdependence should be embraced as an organizing principle of disability support in college. Peer mentorship programs, cross-ability support circles, cooperative learning models, and co-created accommodation plans can all serve as vehicles for enacting interdependence. Institutions must move beyond isolated services and instead create integrated networks of support that recognize students' full social ecosystems. When this shift occurs, students experience not only academic success, but increased confidence, connection, and well-being (Strayhorn, 2018; Wehmeyer et al., 2012).

Redefining success through the lens of interdependence also requires cultural and institutional humility. Colleges must examine how their expectations reflect dominant norms that marginalize disabled and racialized students, and they must co-design new models of support in partnership with those students. Interdependence is not about doing less, it is about doing differently. It is a recognition that access is not granted by a single office or delivered through isolated interventions, but built daily through relationships, trust, and community. Figure 5.1 illustrates how overlapping systems of race, disability, and higher education structures interact to shape students' experiences of access and resistance. When colleges embrace interdependence, they move closer to realizing the transformative potential of disability justice in higher education.

Figure 5.1 – Intersections of Identity and Institutional Barriers in College

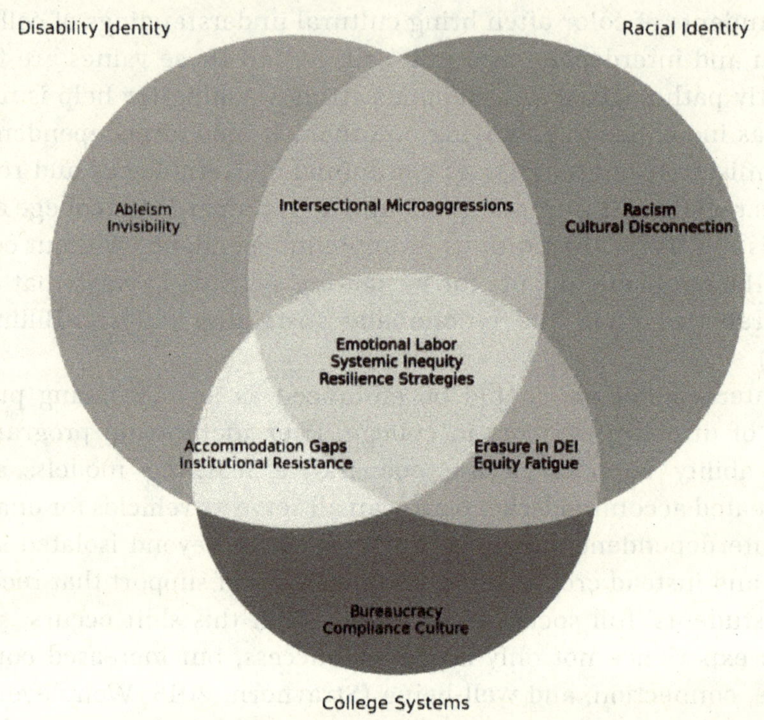

Faculty as Gatekeepers or Allies

While disability services offices play a critical role in coordinating accommodations, the daily educational experience of disabled students is largely shaped by faculty. Professors determine how content is delivered, how flexibility is applied, and how access is either affirmed or denied. Faculty, in many ways, are the gatekeepers of inclusion. Yet despite their influence, many lack the training, resources, or accountability necessary to create truly accessible learning environments. For students with disabilities, particularly those who are also Black, Brown, first-generation, or multilingual, faculty interactions can make the difference between persistence and attrition, belonging and exclusion.

Pedagogical Power: How Faculty Reinforce or Disrupt Ableism

Faculty often wield significant pedagogical authority, but few are taught how their practices may reproduce ableism. Rigid attendance policies, timed exams, participation grades based on verbal speech, and inaccessible readings or media create structural barriers for many students. These practices are not neutral, they reflect assumptions about what a "normal" learner looks like and how learning should occur (Dolmage, 2017). For example, requiring students to perform public speaking without accommodations may inadvertently silence students who stutter, experience social anxiety, or use alternative communication methods.

Disability justice demands that instructors question not only what they teach, but how they teach. Practices like UDL offer frameworks for proactively designing courses that anticipate a range of learning needs without requiring individualized requests (CAST, 2018). UDL encourages faculty to provide multiple ways of engaging with content, demonstrating knowledge, and participating in classroom activities. This approach shifts responsibility from students needing to ask for exceptions to instructors designing with inclusion in mind. As Dolmage (2017) argues, "disability is not the exception, but the expectation."

To truly disrupt ableism in pedagogy, faculty must also interrogate the intersectional dynamics of race, language, and disability in their classrooms. Black and Brown students with disabilities are often read as disruptive, defiant, or unprepared, biases that shape grading, feedback, and instructor-student relationships (Annamma et al., 2013). Disability-affirming pedagogy must be antiracist, culturally sustaining, and aware of the multiple lenses through which student behavior is interpreted.

Faculty Resistance: When Accommodations Are Undermined

Despite federal protections under the ADA and Section 504, faculty noncompliance with accommodations remains a significant problem in higher education. Some instructors openly question whether students "really need" extra time or flexible deadlines, while others quietly ignore accommodation letters. In many cases, students are forced to repeatedly re-explain their needs, monitor follow-through, or confront professors about failures to implement basic adjustments (White et al., 2024).

This pattern places an undue burden on students and reinforces power imbalances in the classroom. It also disproportionately impacts students who are socialized to defer to authority, avoid confrontation, or internalize stigma about asking for help. For disabled students of color, particularly Black and Latinx students, pushing back against faculty noncompliance can carry additional risk, as they may be labeled aggressive or ungrateful (Artiles, 2013; Crenshaw, 1997).

Institutions must take clear steps to address this form of academic gatekeeping. Faculty should be required to complete annual training on disability law and inclusive practices, not as a checkbox, but as an integrated part of their professional development. Additionally, schools must establish streamlined, student-centered reporting mechanisms that protect students from retaliation and ensure timely follow-up. Compliance must be reframed not as an accommodation for a few, but as a shared standard of excellence for all.

Faculty as Allies: Enacting a Culture of Access

While many faculty remain underprepared or resistant, others are actively working to build more inclusive, responsive, and affirming classrooms. These educators collaborate with disability services staff, seek out training, and redesign their syllabi to reflect access as a core value. They recognize that inclusion is not an extra task, but central to their ethical and pedagogical responsibilities (Garland-Thomson, 2011).

Allied faculty practice inclusive teaching by offering flexible deadlines, providing content in multiple formats, and embedding reflective prompts that allow students to name their access needs. They also model vulnerability by sharing their own learning processes, inviting feedback, and co-creating classroom norms with students. In doing so, they signal that learning is relational, not performative, and that access is a collective commitment rather than an individual burden.

Mentorship is also a key dimension of allyship. Faculty who affirm disability identity, provide guidance through institutional systems, and validate student advocacy efforts serve as powerful counterweights to the exclusion many disabled students face. When instructors shift from gatekeepers to allies, they help cultivate an academic culture where difference is not just tolerated, but celebrated.

Campus Initiatives That Work

While many disabled students enter college environments that are unprepared to meet their needs, there are institutions, programs, and initiatives that offer hopeful models for justice-centered change. These examples remind us that when colleges invest in systemic transformation rather than performative inclusion, disabled students are not only able to survive, they are positioned to lead, create, and thrive. Thriving is not the absence of barriers, but the presence of community, visibility, and sustained access. This section highlights innovative practices and campus-based programs that demonstrate what becomes possible when students with disabilities are seen as integral to the life and leadership of higher education.

One promising model is the creation of disability cultural centers (DCCs): spaces that explicitly position disability as an identity, a community, and a source of knowledge, not just a legal status. Unlike traditional disability services offices, which are typically housed in student affairs and focus on accommodation processes, DCCs operate from a cultural and justice-based framework. They provide programming, peer support, mentorship, and advocacy resources while also serving as spaces of resistance to ableism and erasure. Campuses such as Syracuse University and the University of Arizona have led the way in institutionalizing DCCs as hubs for coalition-building across race, gender, and disability (Dolmage, 2017; Jampel, 2018).

Peer mentorship is another transformative approach that helps students move from isolation to connection. Programs like Project REACH at CUNY and Aggie ACHIEVE at Texas A&M pair students with disabilities with trained peer mentors who support them academically, socially, and emotionally. These programs not only reduce stigma around disability but also foster mutual growth and leadership development. When mentoring is framed as interdependent and reciprocal, not charity or saviorism, it allows disabled students to claim space, share strategies, and develop skills critical to college success (Strayhorn, 2018).

Disability-led research collectives and academic centers are also reshaping how higher education understands and responds to access. These initiatives position disabled scholars, not administrators or compliance officers, as the architects of institutional change. For instance, the University of Illinois' Disability Studies program has worked closely with student leaders to revise physical accessibility policies and integrate critical disability theory into core curriculum offerings. When disabled students are engaged as researchers, evaluators, and co-creators of policy, institutions gain insight that is both rigorous and grounded in lived experience (Annamma et al., 2013; Garland-Thomson, 2011).

Programs that work do more than "serve" students with disabilities, they center them in decision-making and ensure that institutional change is driven by those most affected. This requires flexible funding models, leadership pipelines for disabled students, and meaningful accountability structures tied to equity outcomes. It also means moving beyond pilot programs and embedding successful practices into the fabric of the institution. As Harris and Bensimon (2007) argue, transformation occurs not through isolated efforts, but through systemic equity-minded action at every level of the organization.

These models affirm what students with disabilities have long known: Access is not the ceiling, it is the floor. Thriving in college should not be reserved for those who manage to succeed despite their institutions. It should be made possible by institutions that are intentionally built for students of all abilities, cultures, and identities. When colleges commit to justice, not just compliance, they create learning environments where students can fully show up, speak out, and shape the future of higher education.

Conclusion

Navigating college as a student with a disability is not simply about accessing accommodations, it is about asserting presence in institutions that were not built with disability in mind. When students bring intersecting identities shaped by race, class, language, and disability, their journey becomes even more complex. This chapter has examined how campus culture, faculty practices, support systems, and institutional policies can either obstruct or empower disabled students as they seek not only to attend college, but to belong and thrive within it.

Disabled students do not lack potential. What they often lack is access to spaces where their strengths are recognized, their identities are affirmed, and their voices are invited into the fabric of campus life. As we've seen, the barriers students face are not the result of individual shortcomings, but of systemic choices, choices that prioritize compliance over justice, efficiency over humanity, and tradition over transformation.

But the presence of promising programs, student-led movements, and disability-affirming pedagogy reminds us that another path is possible. When campuses are designed with interdependence, cultural responsiveness, and accountability at the center, disabled students are no longer forced to adapt to a system, they help shape a better one. Thriving becomes a collective responsibility, and equity becomes a shared standard rather than an aspiration.

As we turn to the next chapter, we shift focus from institutions to the students themselves, their narratives, strategies, and truths. These stories will illuminate how students resist marginalization, reclaim agency, and imagine new futures beyond access. The power of their voices reminds us that disability justice is not a destination, but a continuous act of redesigning the world with everyone in mind.

References

Annamma, S. A., Connor, D., & Ferri, B. (2013). Untangling the racialization of disabilities: An intersectionality critique across disability models. Dis/ability critical race studies (DisCrit): Theorizing at the intersections of race and dis/ability. *Race Ethnicity and Education, 16*(1), 1–31. https://doi.org/10.1080/13613324.20

12.730511

Artiles, A. J. (2013). Untangling the racialization of disabilities: An intersectionality critique across disability models. *Du Bois Review, 10*(2), 329–347. https://doi.org/10.1017/S1742058X13000270

Bell, D. (1992). The performance of racism. *Sw. UL Rev., 22,* 1103.

CAST. (2018). Universal Design for Learning guidelines version 2.2. https://udlguidelines.cast.org

Crenshaw, K. (1991). *Mapping the Margins: Intersectionality, Identity Politics, and Violence Against Women of Color. Stanford Law Review, 43*(6), 1241–1299.

Crenshaw, K. (1997). Mapping the margins: Intersectionality, identity politics, and violence against. *The Legal Response to Violence Against Women, 5,* 91.

Dolmage, J. T. (2017). *Academic ableism: Disability and higher education.* University of Michigan Press.

Garland-Thomson, R. (2011). *Misfits: A feminist materialist disability concept. Hypatia, 26*(3), 591–609. https://doi.org/10.1111/j.1527-2001.2011.01206.x

Harris III, F., & Bensimon, E. M. (2007). The equity scorecard: A collaborative approach to assess and respond to racial/ethnic disparities in student outcomes. *New Directions for Student Services, 2007*(120), 77–84.

Harry, B., & Klingner, J. K. (2006). *Why are so many minority students in special education? Understanding race and disability in schools.* New York, NY: Teachers College Press.

Jampel, C. (2018). Intersections of disability justice, racial justice and environmental justice. *Environmental Sociology, 4*(1), 122–135.

Ladson-Billings, G. (2021). *Critical race theory in education: A scholar's journey.* Teachers College Press.

Mazzotti, V. L., Rowe, D. A., Kwiatek, S., Voggt, A., Chang, W.H., Fowler, C. H., Poppen, M., Sinclair, J., & Test, D. W. (2021). Secondary transition predictors of postschool success: An update to the research base. *Career Development and Transition for Exceptional Individuals, 44*(1), 47–64. https://doi.org/10.1177/2165143420959793

Phillips, B. A., Fortney, S., & Swafford, L. (2019). College students' social perceptions toward individuals with intellectual disability. *Journal of Disability Policy Studies, 30*(1), 3–10.

Strayhorn, T. L. (2018). *College students' sense of belonging: A key to educational success for all students* (2nd ed.). Routledge.

Wehmeyer, M. L., Shogren, K. A., Palmer, S. B., Williams-Diehm, K. L., Little, T. D., & Boulton, A. (2012). The impact of the self-determined learning model of instruction on student self-determination. *Exceptional Children, 78*(2), 135–153.

White, L. M., D. Adams, K. Simpson, & S. A. Malone. 2024. "Transitioning on from Secondary School for Autistic Students: A Systematic Review." Autism in Adulthood. https://doi.org/10.1089/aut.2023.0193

CHAPTER 6

Independent Living and Life Skills Development

For students with disabilities, preparing for life beyond college is not just about earning a degree, it is about navigating the everyday realities of adulthood with agency, confidence, and support. Independent living is often framed in terms of self-care, budgeting, transportation, and decision-making, but these skills are not developed in a vacuum. They are shaped by cultural values, systemic barriers, and access to inclusive environments. For disabled students who also come from historically marginalized communities, building life skills requires more than individual preparation; it demands intentional support structures that affirm identity, promote autonomy, and recognize interdependence as a legitimate and powerful framework. This chapter explores the competencies, supports, and mindsets needed to equip students with disabilities for meaningful adult lives, on their terms.

Redefining Independence in Context

Challenging the Myth of Individual Independence

In the dominant culture of Western education and rehabilitation, independence is often portrayed as the ultimate goal for students with disabilities. This vision of adulthood emphasizes self-sufficiency, detachment from family support, and the ability to navigate all systems alone. Yet this notion is deeply rooted in ableist, capitalist, and white middle-class ideals that fail to account for the cultural and structural realities many students face (Dolmage, 2017; Ladson-Billings, 2021). For disabled students, especially those from Black, Brown, immigrant, or low-income communities, interdependence is not a weakness, it is a survival strategy and cultural value (Invalid, 2017). Families and communities often provide critical support across the lifespan, offering emotional, financial, and caregiving networks that reflect traditions of collective responsibility. Defining success through the lens of individualism erases these strengths and places unfair burdens on students to conform to normative expectations of adulthood.

Disability justice advocates have long challenged the binary thinking that separates independence from dependence. Instead, they propose a framework of interdependence, where people are supported in ways that affirm dignity, autonomy, and connection (Invalid, 2017). This model recognizes that all people, disabled or not, rely on one another to live full lives, and that support should not be stigmatized. For example, using a personal care assistant, relying on assistive technology, or living with family beyond age 18 does not make someone "less adult." These forms of support are legitimate and often necessary responses to a world that is inaccessible by design (Garland-Thomson, 2011). By redefining independence, we can create transition plans and educational goals that validate diverse ways of living and thriving.

Cultural and Structural Perspectives on Autonomy

In many cultures, adulthood is not marked by leaving home or managing life alone, but by contributing to the well-being of the family or community. Students from immigrant households, for example, may be expected to live with and care for elders, help with translation and finances, or prioritize collective goals over individual ones (Harry & Klingner, 2014). When schools and service providers ignore these values, they risk labeling culturally aligned behavior as deficient or immature. Transition programs must understand that independence looks different across families and cultures, and they must partner with families to create goals that reflect students' realities. Autonomy should not mean disconnection, but the ability to make informed choices within the context of one's identity, needs, and cultural framework (Wehmeyer et al., 2012). Respecting autonomy means affirming students' right to define success in ways that honor both personal agency and collective belonging.

Barriers to independence are not always rooted in personal readiness, but in systemic inequities that limit students' access to safe housing, reliable transportation, and healthcare. A student who cannot find affordable, accessible housing may be forced to stay in unsafe conditions, not because they are unprepared, but because society has failed to create viable options. Similarly, students with disabilities who live in rural areas or face discrimination in housing and employment may experience limited options through no fault of their own (Artiles, 2013). A justice-centered approach to independent living must recognize and address these structural barriers. Independence must be reframed not as a test of individual ability, but as a question of what supports and systems are available. When the conversation shifts in this way, it becomes clear that the problem is not the student's lack of readiness, it is society's lack of access.

Core Domains of Independent Living

Developing independent living skills is essential for young adults with disabilities to fully participate in community life beyond secondary and postsecondary education. These competencies extend beyond academics and influence every aspect of adult identity, stability, and autonomy. For students from historically marginalized communities, the path to independence is shaped not only by individual ability but also by access to opportunity, systemic inequities, and culturally informed expectations. The development of life skills must be situated within a justice framework that addresses the social determinants of independence, including racism, ableism, economic injustice, and policy design. In this section, I examine four core domains, housing, transportation, health and wellness, and financial literacy, and their significance in preparing students for successful transitions into adulthood.

Stability, Accessibility, and Belonging

Safe, affordable, and accessible housing is a fundamental right, yet it remains one of the greatest barriers to independence for disabled young adults. The national shortage of accessible housing disproportionately impacts students with mobility, sensory, or cognitive disabilities and is even more acute for those who are also low income or people of color (da Silveira et al., 2025). Many students graduate from high school or college with no knowledge of how to apply for housing vouchers, navigate tenant rights, or access home modifications. Others live in communities with limited housing stock that meets the Americans with Disabilities Act (ADA) standards, forcing them to compromise on location, safety, or autonomy. Moreover, housing insecurity intersects with disability status in damaging ways, as students without stable housing may forgo medical care, employment, or further education (Friedman & VanPuymbrouck, 2019). Transition programs must prepare students not only to live independently, but to advocate for housing justice as a condition for community inclusion.

Students need direct instruction in applying for housing, understanding leases, communicating with landlords, and securing financial assistance. Schools should partner with local housing authorities, disability rights centers, and community-based organizations to provide realistic planning tools, particularly for those aging out of foster care, group homes, or institutional settings. Instruction must also incorporate conversations around cultural expectations regarding multigenerational housing and family interdependence. For some students, independent housing is not the desired outcome; instead, co-housing or living with extended family may better reflect their values and support needs. Programs must honor this diversity and avoid imposing narrow definitions of "successful living." Preparing students for independence means equipping them with information and options, not predetermined outcomes.

Mobility as Access and Liberation

Access to reliable, accessible transportation determines whether students with disabilities can work, continue their education, attend medical appointments, and participate in community life. Yet for many, transportation systems are unreliable, unsafe, or entirely unavailable. Paratransit services often require advanced scheduling, have long wait times, and are inconsistently available across counties and municipalities (National Council on Disability, 2015). Public transportation systems frequently fail to meet the access standards set by the ADA, with broken elevators, inaccessible stops, and discriminatory operator practices disproportionately impacting Black and Brown disabled riders (Pineda, 2020). Rural students and those in transit deserts face compounded challenges, often depending on family members or being entirely homebound. These transportation inequities are not incidental, they are manifestations of ableism and economic injustice embedded in public infrastructure.

Transition planning must address transportation explicitly and early. Students should learn how to read transit maps, plan routes, access reduced fare programs, and navigate ride-share alternatives safely. Instruction should include safety protocols, rights under the ADA, and how to advocate for more accessible systems. Collaboration with community mobility training programs and disability transportation coalitions can provide experiential learning that builds confidence and self-determination. Educators must also recognize that transportation is a racial equity issue and advocate for infrastructure that centers the needs of multiply marginalized disabled people. Without equitable mobility, independence remains a hollow promise.

Health and Wellness: Accessing Care, Building Literacy

Managing one's health is a cornerstone of independent adulthood, yet many students with disabilities leave school with little experience navigating the healthcare system. Transitioning from pediatric to adult care often brings abrupt shifts in provider relationships, insurance coverage, and service availability. For students with chronic illnesses, mental health diagnoses, or developmental disabilities, accessing consistent care can be overwhelming, especially when providers lack disability competence or cultural responsiveness. Students of color report additional layers of mistrust, discrimination, and misdiagnosis in medical settings, reinforcing longstanding disparities in health outcomes (Artiga et al., 2020). Health literacy, self-advocacy, and systems navigation must be taught as life skills, not left to trial and error.

Curricula should include scheduling appointments, managing prescriptions, understanding insurance forms, and communicating with healthcare professionals. Students must also be taught how to track symptoms, monitor wellness goals, and recognize when to seek help. Schools should collaborate with local health clinics, mental health providers, and Medicaid waiver programs to ensure students understand the resources available in their communities. Teaching these skills is not only a matter of access—it is an act of survival. Without adequate preparation, students may delay treatment, forgo necessary care, or suffer avoidable health crises that derail their postsecondary and life goals. Disability justice demands a model of care that is preventive, person centered, and embedded within transition services.

Economic Justice and Lifelong Skills

Financial literacy is a key area where students with disabilities often experience systemic exclusion. Many students graduate without basic knowledge of how to manage a budget, open a bank account, pay bills, or avoid predatory financial practices. For students receiving Supplemental Security Income (SSI) or Medicaid, the complexity of benefits systems adds an additional layer of difficulty; earning too much can result in losing essential supports, which disincentivizes work and independence (Taylor et al., 2023). Students from low-income households may also lack access to trusted financial role models, multilingual resources, or culturally relevant instruction. Without targeted support, students are left to navigate financial adulthood in systems that were not built for them.

Transition programs should incorporate financial literacy instruction that includes budgeting, saving, responsible credit use, and public benefits navigation. Educators should collaborate with financial counselors who understand disability-related income rules and assistive technology funding. Students also need culturally relevant examples, such as supporting family members or contributing to community obligations, woven into financial goal-setting.

Teaching financial literacy through a justice lens means demystifying systems, addressing structural inequities, and preparing students to assert control over their economic futures. Table 6.1 highlights key areas such as housing, healthcare, self-advocacy, and financial management, along with practices that center equity and student empowerment. Financial independence is not simply about numbers, it is about empowerment, access, and informed choice.

Table 6.1 – Core Domains of Independent Living and Justice-Oriented Strategies

Domain	Common Barriers	Justice-Oriented Strategies
Housing	Lack of affordable, accessible housing; limited knowledge of housing rights	Teach tenant rights, connect with local housing authorities, honor multigenerational preferences
Transportation	Inaccessible infrastructure, unreliable paratransit, rural transit deserts	Partner with mobility training programs, advocate for racial and disability transit equity
Health and Wellness	Gaps in adult healthcare, mistrust, cultural incompetence in providers	Teach health literacy, partner with clinics, promote preventive and person-centered care
Financial Literacy	Systemic exclusion, benefits cliffs, lack of culturally relevant instruction	Embed public benefits instruction, use culturally affirming budgeting and saving practices
Executive Function	Assumed knowledge, unstructured environments, cultural disconnect	Teach planning and time management with visual supports and assistive tech
Daily Living Skills	Social stigma, lack of instruction, vulnerability in the community	Provide real-world learning and trauma-informed instruction, emphasize safety and dignity
Technology Access	Digital divide, lack of training, surveillance concerns	Frame tech as a right, teach digital literacy, ensure culturally responsive access

Building Executive Function and Daily Living Skills

Executive functioning and daily living skills are essential for navigating the complexities of adult life, yet these areas are often underemphasized in transition planning. Students with disabilities, particularly those with ADHD, autism, or learning disabilities, may struggle with organization, time management, planning, or self-monitoring, not due to a lack of motivation, but because of neurological differences that require specific strategies and supports. Similarly, daily living skills such as hygiene, food preparation, and personal safety are too often assumed rather than explicitly taught. These competencies are foundational not only to independent living but also to building self-confidence and reducing dependency on crisis interventions. For students with multiple marginalized identities, skill-building must be responsive to cultural context, access barriers, and individual learning preferences. This section examines how schools and postsecondary institutions can effectively support executive function and daily living development through inclusive, affirming, and practical instruction.

Executive Function: Planning, Organization, and Time Management

Executive function challenges can affect a student's ability to prioritize tasks, initiate activities, manage deadlines, or regulate emotions, all of which are critical for success in adult life. In higher education and employment contexts, these skills are often unspoken expectations that, when unmet, result in academic penalties or job loss. Students from under-resourced schools may not have received structured instruction in executive functioning, leaving them at a disadvantage in more demanding environments (DuPaul et al., 2021). Transition programs must prioritize building these skills through modeling, guided practice, visual supports, and assistive technology. Strategies such as digital calendars, visual schedules, task breakdowns, and regular check-ins can help students build sustainable routines. Instruction should affirm students' strengths and avoid framing executive differences as failures, instead positioning these skills as learnable and adaptable.

Instructional supports must also consider cultural and linguistic responsiveness. For example, time management may look different in collectivist or interdependent cultures where obligations to family or community take precedence over rigid deadlines. Educators should create flexible systems that validate students' lived realities while still promoting goal-setting, accountability, and agency. The inclusion of mentors, particularly those with shared experiences of disability and cultural identity, can provide students with both guidance and affirmation. When executive function is addressed in affirming and structured ways, students are more likely to meet adult expectations with confidence, self-awareness, and increasing autonomy.

Daily Living Skills: Hygiene, Nutrition, and Safety

Daily living skills are foundational to independent adulthood, yet they are often overlooked in academic transition planning. These include personal hygiene, appropriate dress, meal preparation, grocery shopping, household cleaning, and safe community engagement. For students with intellectual or developmental disabilities, explicit instruction in these areas can mean the difference between full community participation and social isolation. Without these skills, students may be more vulnerable to health risks, exploitation, or housing instability. Programs must avoid assuming that these skills are learned at home and instead provide structured, judgment-free learning environments to build competency (Henninger & Taylor, 2014).

Teaching daily living skills should incorporate both simulation and real-world practice. Schools can partner with community organizations, independent living centers, or on-campus living labs to provide opportunities for hands-on learning. Instruction should be trauma informed and affirming, recognizing that some students may have experienced stigma, control, or institutionalization related to their disabilities and bodies. Topics like personal boundaries, consent, and public versus private behavior must also be taught with cultural sensitivity and age-appropriate language. Life skills instruction is not about enforcing compliance with dominant norms of adulthood, it's about equipping students to live with agency, dignity, and safety.

Technology as a Tool for Independence

Technology can serve as both a bridge and a barrier to independence. For students with executive function challenges, assistive technology can support memory, organization, and communication. Tools such as reminder apps, screen readers, GPS navigation, budgeting software, or smart home devices allow students to engage with the world in more autonomous and efficient ways. However, access to technology is not equitably distributed, and some students, particularly those from low-income families or rural areas, may lack the infrastructure, training, or internet access needed to benefit from these supports (Pew Research Center, 2021). Institutions must ensure that technology instruction is part of transition planning and is framed not as a privilege, but as a right.

Training in technology should not be limited to device use but should also include digital literacy, privacy protections, and skills for identifying scams or online misinformation. Students must understand how to use technology safely and strategically across different aspects of life, communication, banking, transportation, academics, and social connection. Culturally responsive practices are especially important here, as not all students may be comfortable with or exposed to technology in the same way. Technology must be a tool of empowerment, not surveillance or standardization. When integrated thoughtfully, digital tools can help students express independence on their own terms.

Cultural Considerations and Family Expectations

Transition planning for independent living often overlooks the cultural, familial, and community contexts that shape how students with disabilities define adulthood. Too frequently, schools approach transition as a linear path toward complete self-sufficiency, rooted in Western, individualistic ideals. This framing ignores the deeply relational nature of decision-making, care, and identity formation in many communities. For students from Black, Indigenous, Latinx, Asian, immigrant, or multilingual backgrounds, family and culture play central roles in shaping adult roles and expectations.

Independence may not mean moving out or managing every aspect of life alone, it may mean contributing to the household, sharing responsibilities, or making interdependent decisions. When educational systems fail to understand these dynamics, they risk labeling culturally grounded behavior as inappropriate, immature, or dependent.

Honoring Family as a Source of Strength

In many communities, particularly among students of color, family is a core site of resilience, support, and cultural identity. Parents, siblings, extended kin, and spiritual elders often play active roles in decision-making and caregiving, including in adulthood. Yet transition planning processes often marginalize families or expect them to "step back" once students reach a certain age. This assumption can be especially harmful for students with disabilities who rely on family members not only for practical support, but for emotional and cultural grounding (Harry & Klingner, 2014). Schools must shift from seeing family involvement as a barrier to independence to understanding it as an asset that can be harnessed for long-term success. Culturally responsive planning includes active listening, collaborative goal-setting, and validating intergenerational models of adulthood.

In some cases, students with disabilities may not wish to live independently from their families. Instead, they may envision adulthood as contributing to a multigenerational household or caregiving network. Educators should not pathologize this choice or assume it reflects a lack of readiness. Autonomy can coexist with connection, and planning should reflect students' preferences, not a prescriptive notion of what adulthood should look like. Valuing family participation means co-creating transition goals that align with both the student's and the family's cultural and practical realities. When families are engaged as collaborators, outcomes are more sustainable, affirming, and just.

Navigating Cultural Stigma and System Distrust

Despite the strengths of family networks, some families may hesitate to fully engage with disability-related services due to stigma, shame, or prior negative experiences with schools and systems. In many cultures, disability is not openly discussed, or it is viewed through religious, spiritual, or community-specific lenses that differ from Western medical models. Families may also fear that involvement with transition services will lead to loss of control, increased surveillance, or unwanted pressure on their child to conform to mainstream expectations. For families who have experienced racism, xenophobia, or exclusion in school settings, trust in educators and institutions may be low (Artiga et al., 2020). Culturally responsive transition planning must address these realities with humility, patience, and respect.

To bridge these gaps, schools must invest in relationships, not just outreach. This includes using interpreters, hiring culturally representative staff, conducting meetings in community settings, and adapting materials to match families' preferred modes of communication. Educators should ask families about their values, roles, and hopes, not simply tell them what to expect. Cultural brokers, family liaisons, and peer mentors can serve as powerful connectors between home and school. Building trust requires a long-term commitment, not one-time events or checklists. When families feel seen, heard, and respected, they are more likely to participate fully and authentically in the planning process.

Culturally Sustaining Instruction and Program Design

Culturally sustaining pedagogy recognizes that students' identities, traditions, and worldviews are not barriers to success, they are sources of insight and strength. In the context of transition, this means designing instruction and services that affirm students' languages, spiritual beliefs, community ties, and cultural understandings of disability and adulthood. For example, teaching life skills should incorporate culturally familiar foods, financial practices, and household norms. Mentorship and peer support programs should reflect the diversity of the students they serve, ensuring that students can see themselves in leadership roles and future possibilities (Paris & Alim, 2017).

Program design must also reflect the lived realities of immigrant, multilingual, and racially marginalized students with disabilities. This includes offering flexible pathways, building in translation and family engagement as standard practices, and creating transition goals that reflect a range of postsecondary options, not just traditional college or independent living. Schools must challenge deficit-based narratives that frame students' cultural practices as obstacles. Instead, they must design programs that nourish and expand students' full identities. Culturally sustaining transition planning is not about inclusion, it is about co-creation, respect, and transformation.

Instructional Practices That Promote Life Readiness

Preparing students for adult life requires intentional, inclusive, and culturally grounded instruction that extends beyond academics. Too often, life skills and independent living competencies are treated as peripheral or "soft skills," rather than core outcomes of K-12 and postsecondary education. This marginalization disproportionately harms students with disabilities, especially those from historically excluded communities, who may not receive explicit instruction in navigating systems, building autonomy, or sustaining well-being. Instructional strategies must reflect a holistic understanding of readiness: one that integrates academic content with practical, relational, and identity-affirming learning. This section outlines four practices that promote authentic life readiness and equip students to navigate adulthood on their own terms.

Embedding Life Skills in IEPs and Transition Goals

The Individualized Education Plan (IEP) is a critical vehicle for preparing students with disabilities for life beyond school. However, in many cases, transition goals are vague, compliance driven, or disconnected from the student's lived experience. Embedding life skills into IEPs means intentionally incorporating measurable, individualized, and culturally responsive goals that address housing, employment, health care navigation, and community engagement. For example, rather than simply stating that a student will "live independently," an IEP might specify that the student will "demonstrate the ability to apply for and maintain a housing voucher, with support, by age 19." This level of specificity allows educators, families, and service providers to coordinate efforts around real-world tasks and empower students with relevant skills.

Effective IEPs also reflect student voice and family input. Students must be supported to identify and articulate their own goals, preferences, and visions of adulthood. This can be facilitated through student-led IEP meetings, vision statements, and multimedia self-advocacy portfolios. For families, especially those from nondominant cultural backgrounds, schools should create meaningful opportunities to co-construct transition plans that honor interdependence and collective values. IEP teams must avoid using standardized checklists that center white, middle-class norms of adulthood and instead ask: What does success look like for this student in their cultural, community, and economic context?

To build capacity among educators, professional development must be provided on how to write life-centered IEP goals that are both practical and affirming. This includes training on co-writing with students, connecting with adult service providers, and using community-based instruction as data. When IEPs center real-world application, they become powerful tools for preparation, not just documentation. Embedding life readiness into IEPs requires a shift from compliance to collaboration, from bureaucracy to belonging.

Community-Based and Experiential Learning

Real-world learning is essential for building life skills. Community-based instruction (CBI) allows students to practice budgeting in grocery stores, learn transportation planning on public buses, or rehearse job interviews in workplace settings. These opportunities are especially critical for students who learn best through hands-on experiences, contextual modeling, or repetition across environments. Yet access to high-quality CBI is often unequal. Students in underfunded schools, particularly those in rural areas or communities of color, may have fewer partnerships with local businesses, transportation services, or healthcare providers. Schools must be proactive in cultivating inclusive partnerships that reflect students' neighborhoods, cultural institutions, and daily realities.

Experiential learning should also be embedded across academic subjects, not confined to "special" classes. For example, math classes can incorporate real-world budgeting, while English classes can support resume writing and communication skills. By embedding transition outcomes across disciplines, schools affirm that life readiness is not an extracurricular concern, it is an academic imperative. Interdisciplinary collaboration is key. General education teachers, special educators, related service providers, and community mentors should co-design units that prepare students for both diploma and daily life.

Additionally, experiential learning must account for student safety, agency, and dignity. For many disabled students, navigating community spaces has historically meant exposure to surveillance, stigma, or institutional control. Educators must prepare students not only to function in these environments but to assert their rights, advocate for themselves, and assess risk. Justice-oriented CBI empowers students to move through the world with confidence and critical consciousness, not just compliance.

Collaborative Instruction Across Systems

Promoting life readiness requires coordinated instruction that bridges education, health, workforce, and social service systems. Too often, transition planning ends at the school's doorstep, leaving students and families to navigate fragmented services alone. Educators should partner with vocational rehabilitation agencies, independent living centers, Medicaid waiver providers, and housing authorities to integrate real-world content into instruction. These partnerships can provide guest speakers, shadowing opportunities, joint training sessions, and individualized coaching for students preparing to age out of school-based services. When done well, interagency collaboration allows instruction to extend beyond the classroom and into the structures students will rely on in adulthood.

One effective strategy is the use of "transition fairs" or "life readiness expos," where students and families meet directly with service providers, complete applications, and learn about available supports. However, these events must be accessible, culturally responsive, and intentionally inclusive of students with complex support needs. Translation services, transportation assistance, and one-on-one navigation support should be built into the planning process.

More importantly, collaboration should not be limited to events. It must be embedded in curriculum, reflected in shared data systems, and sustained through formalized partnerships and memoranda of understanding.

Instructional teams must also advocate for systemic alignment. For example, when a student receives training on medication management in school but cannot transfer those skills due to lack of coordination with adult care providers, instruction loses its impact. Cross-system instructional planning ensures that what is taught in school translates into sustainable adult outcomes. It also reinforces to students that their futures matter beyond graduation day, that institutions are working together to support their journey, not leaving them to piece it together alone.

Barriers to Access and Opportunities for Change

While students with disabilities are often asked to demonstrate "readiness" for adulthood, it is society that frequently fails to be ready for them. The systems that claim to support transition, education, healthcare, housing, transportation, and workforce development are fragmented, under-resourced, and misaligned with the lived experiences of multiply marginalized youth. These barriers are not merely logistical; they are rooted in ableism, racism, and economic injustice that restrict access and reinforce dependence. Understanding these structural constraints is essential for designing effective transition supports that empower rather than penalize students. This section examines five major barriers and highlights opportunities for educational and community systems to respond with equity and accountability.

Underfunded and Inaccessible Adult Services

Many students graduate from school-based special education systems only to discover that adult services are far less comprehensive, coordinated, or accessible. Medicaid waiver programs often have long waiting lists, eligibility requirements are inconsistent across states, and services vary significantly by geography and disability label. Students with high support needs are especially vulnerable to falling through service gaps due to bureaucratic red tape and lack of coordinated case management. Moreover, adult services are often siloed, housing supports are disconnected from vocational training, and healthcare access is rarely integrated with mental health support or transportation planning. This disjointed infrastructure creates confusion, delays, and an over-reliance on family support, disproportionately impacting low-income and first-generation students (Friedman & VanPuymbrouck, 2019).

Schools must recognize that transition does not end at graduation; it requires preparing students to advocate for services in adult systems and empowering them to navigate eligibility processes with support. Instruction in public benefits, supported decision-making, and advocacy must begin early and be reinforced across multiple grade levels. Partnerships with service providers should not be an afterthought; they should be formalized through shared planning, information exchanges, and co-taught sessions. When systems fail to connect, students are forced to carry the burden. When systems collaborate, students are affirmed as full members of the adult world.

Discrimination in Housing, Employment, and Healthcare

Disabled students of color face intersecting forms of discrimination that limit their access to housing, employment, and healthcare—three pillars of independent living. In housing, ableist design, affordability crises, and discriminatory rental practices often exclude individuals with disabilities from safe and stable homes (da Silveira et al., 2025). In employment, hiring discrimination, workplace inaccessibility, and fear of benefit loss continue to prevent full participation in the labor force, especially for young adults who are multiply marginalized (Taylor et al., 2023). Healthcare settings can be alienating, dismissive, or outright hostile, particularly for disabled students who are also navigating racism, linguistic barriers, or mental health stigma (Artiga et al., 2020).

Educators cannot remove these barriers alone, but they can equip students with the skills and tools to resist them. This includes teaching students their legal rights, how to file complaints, where to find advocacy organizations, and how to build networks of peer and community support. Schools must also engage in systems-level advocacy, pushing policymakers to expand protections and enforce antidiscrimination laws across sectors. Life readiness must include the capacity to navigate, not just survive, systems that are too often built on exclusion. Thriving requires not just personal growth, but public accountability.

Structural Racism and Policy Fragmentation

The intersection of race, class, and disability often results in compounded inequities, particularly when policies are implemented unevenly or not at all. Students of color with disabilities are less likely to be referred to adult services, more likely to be placed in segregated educational settings, and less likely to receive coordinated transition support. Many schools serving Black and Brown communities are underfunded, oversurveilled, and overburdened, limiting their capacity to provide robust transition planning. Additionally, because federal policies like the Individuals with Disabilities Education Act (IDEA) do not require implementation beyond age 21, transition services often disappear just as adult life begins. Policy fragmentation across IDEA, Section 504, the ADA, and Medicaid results in disjointed protections that vary not only by state, but by zip code.

To counteract these disparities, equity must be written into the structure of transition services. States and districts should be required to report disaggregated transition outcomes by race, disability category, income, and language background, and to act on disparities with targeted resources. Educators, community leaders, and families must be included in shaping the policies that govern transition, ensuring that those most affected are not excluded from the decisions that impact them. Equity is not achieved through access alone; it requires restructuring systems to be accountable for the outcomes they produce.

Thriving Beyond Systems

Independent living is often framed in terms of navigating existing systems, housing, healthcare, employment, and education. But for many disabled students, especially those who experience multiple forms of marginalization, these systems have historically excluded, harmed, or ignored them. Thriving beyond systems means preparing students not only to survive within existing institutions, but to build alternatives, shape community, and affirm their right to define adulthood on their own terms. It requires shifting from compliance to liberation, from deficit to possibility. This section explores three interrelated pathways—self-determination, peer and community networks, and disability-led models of support—that allow students to thrive outside and beyond traditional systems.

Self-Determination as a Lifelong Practice

Self-determination is not just about making isolated decisions, it is about developing the skills, confidence, and agency to shape one's life, advocate for one's rights, and pursue meaningful goals. For students with disabilities, cultivating self-determination is essential to independent living, but it cannot be reduced to a checklist of behaviors or one-size-fits-all programs. It must be rooted in identity, culture, and relationship. Students need ongoing opportunities to practice choice-making, problem-solving, and goal-setting in environments that support, rather than punish, their growth. This includes learning how to ask for help, navigate complex institutions, and adjust plans without shame or failure. Self-determination, when taught with cultural humility and relational support, becomes a liberatory tool that students can carry throughout their lives (Wehmeyer et al., 2012).

Instruction in self-determination must begin early and continue beyond high school. Educators can use models such as the Self-Determined Learning Model of Instruction (SDLMI) to teach students how to set personal goals, evaluate progress, and reflect on their growth. Importantly, these lessons must be adapted for students with varying communication styles, learning preferences, and cognitive profiles. Teachers should also work closely with families to ensure that opportunities for self-determination are reinforced at home and across contexts. When students are taught to recognize their power and given opportunities to exercise it meaningfully, they are better equipped to advocate for themselves and others in adulthood. True preparation for independence centers not just skills, but the belief that one's voice matters.

Peer Networks and Collective Empowerment

While systems may fail to provide adequate support, peer networks can offer a powerful alternative. Connecting students with others who share similar experiences, challenges, and aspirations creates a sense of belonging that is essential to well-being. Peer mentoring, cross-disability support groups, and cultural affinity spaces allow students to build social capital and emotional resilience. These relationships affirm that students are not alone and that their struggles are part of broader systemic patterns, not personal shortcomings. Schools can facilitate these connections by creating leadership pathways for disabled students, funding student-led organizations, and integrating peer supports into transition planning.

Peer networks also serve as incubators for collective problem-solving and activism. Through these communities, students learn to navigate challenges together, share resources, and build coalitions across lines of race, language, disability, and gender. This collective approach shifts the narrative from "how can I adapt to systems" to "how can we transform systems to meet our needs?" Institutions should actively support and resource these networks as essential components of transition success, not extracurriculars. Empowerment grows when students are surrounded by others who believe in their potential and affirm their experiences. Peer relationships are not just social, they are infrastructural.

Disability-Led Models of Interdependence

Thriving beyond systems also means reimagining what support can look like when it is designed by, for, and with disabled people. Across the country, disability justice organizers are developing alternative models of housing, care, and community that center interdependence, accessibility, and liberation. These include cooperative living spaces, mutual aid networks, community-based personal care collectives, and disability cultural centers. Such models reject institutionalization and charity-based frameworks in favor of equity, dignity, and shared power (Invalid, 2017). Introducing students to these models expands their vision of what is possible beyond compliance-based adulthood.

Educators can invite guest speakers, arrange site visits, and use project-based learning to help students explore disability-led spaces and practices. These experiences challenge dominant narratives about success, adulthood, and independence, offering students the language and tools to build futures grounded in justice. They also encourage students to see themselves not just as service recipients, but as contributors, leaders, and architects of change. When students are given access to community-rooted alternatives, they are less likely to internalize institutional failures as personal ones. They are more likely to imagine, and pursue, futures that reflect their full humanity.

Conclusion

Independent living is not a destination but a lifelong journey shaped by culture, identity, access, and opportunity. For students with disabilities, particularly those from historically marginalized communities, thriving in adulthood is not simply about learning how to live alone, it is about learning how to live freely, fully, and on their own terms. This chapter has pushed back against narrow, ableist definitions of independence and instead embraced a more expansive, interdependent vision of adulthood. By centering students' lived experiences, affirming their cultural values, and teaching practical life skills through inclusive, community-rooted instruction, we move closer to systems that support real freedom and choice.

Preparing students for life beyond graduation means addressing not only what they need to learn, but what society needs to unlearn. The work of transition is not about fixing students, it is about redesigning the environments, expectations, and supports around them. When we shift our attention from compliance to care, from surveillance to solidarity, we create the conditions in which young people with disabilities can grow, lead, and define their own futures. Independent living is not about doing everything alone, it is about building lives that are connected, meaningful, and just.

As we look ahead to the next chapter, we turn our focus to another critical dimension of postsecondary success: employment. From navigating workplace discrimination to accessing meaningful career pathways, the chapter will explore how students with disabilities can move beyond exclusion and into empowered, equitable participation in the workforce.

References

Artiga, S., Orgera, K., & Pham, O. (2020). *Disparities in health and health care: Five key questions and answers.* Kaiser Family Foundation. https://www.kff.org

Artiles, A. J. (2013). Untangling the racialization of disabilities: An intersectionality critique across disability models. *Du Bois Review: Social Science Research on Race, 10*(2), 329–347. https://doi.org/10.1017/S1742058X13000270

da Silveira, J., de Oliveira, R. R., Schmitt, B. D., & Seron, B. B. (2025). Social Determinants of Health in the Lives of People with Disability. *Disability, CBR & Inclusive Development, 36*(1), 85–102.

Dolmage, J. T. (2017). *Academic ableism: Disability and higher education.* University of Michigan Press.

DuPaul, G. J., Gormley, M. J., Anastopoulos, A. D., Weyandt, L. L., Labban, J., Sass, A. J., ... & Postler, K. B. (2021). Academic trajectories of college students with and without ADHD: Predictors of four-year outcomes. *Journal of Clinical Child & Adolescent Psychology, 50*(6), 828–843.

Friedman, C., & VanPuymbrouck, L. (2019). The relationship between disability prejudice and Medicaid home and community-based services spending. *Disability and Health Journal, 12*(3), 359–365.

Garland-Thomson, R. (2011). Misfits: A feminist materialist disability concept. *Hypatia, 26*(3), 591–609. https://doi.org/10.1111/j.1527-2001.2011.01206.x

Harry, B., & Klingner, J. (2014). *Why are so many minority students in special education?: Understanding race and disability in schools.* Teachers College Press.

Henninger, N. A., & Taylor, J. L. (2014). Family perspectives on a successful transition to adulthood for individuals with disabilities. *Mental Retardation,* 52(2), 98–111.

Ladson-Billings, G. (2021). *Critical race theory in education: A scholar's journey.* Teachers College Press.

National Council on Disability. (2015). *Transportation update: Where we've gone and what we've learned.* https://www.ncd.gov

Paris, D., & Alim, H. S. (2017). *Culturally sustaining pedagogies: Teaching and learning for justice in a changing world.* Teachers College Press.

Pew Research Center. (2021). *Internet/broadband fact sheet.* https://www.pewresearch.org/internet/fact-sheet/internet-broadband

Pineda, V. S. (2020). *Building the inclusive city: Governance, access, and the urban transformation of Dubai* (p. 169). Springer Nature.

Sins Invalid. 2016. Skin, Tooth, and Bone–The Basis of Movement Is Our People: A Disability Justice Primer. Sins Invalid. San Francisco, CA: Dancer's Group. https://www.flipcause.com/secure/reward_step2/OTMxNQ==/3489

Taylor, J. P., Avellone, L., Wehman, P., & Brooke, V. (2023). The efficacy of competitive integrated employment versus segregated employment for persons with disabilities: A systematic review. *Journal of Vocational Rehabilitation, 58*(1), 63–78.

Wehmeyer, M. L., Shogren, K. A., Palmer, S. B., Williams-Diehm, K. L., Little, T. D., & Boulton, A. (2012). The impact of the self-determined learning model of instruction on student self-determination. *Exceptional Children, 78*(2), 135–153.

PART III

Overcoming Barriers and Expanding Opportunities

CHAPTER 7

Addressing Ableism and Systemic Barriers in Postsecondary Institutions

Although access to college has expanded in recent decades, students with disabilities continue to confront ableism, exclusion, and institutional neglect across postsecondary settings. These challenges are not incidental, they are structural, embedded in policies, practices, and assumptions that define who belongs and who succeeds. From inaccessible classrooms and punitive attendance policies to stigmatizing accommodation processes and lack of disability representation, ableism shows up in both overt and subtle ways. As discussed in Chapter 6, many of the barriers that students face in developing independent living skills are mirrored in the institutional norms of higher education, where autonomy is often defined through able-bodied standards and systemic supports are inconsistently applied. For students who also identify as Black, Indigenous, Latinx, low income, queer, or multilingual, these barriers are compounded by intersecting forms of oppression. This chapter examines how ableism operates within higher education and explores strategies for dismantling systemic barriers in pursuit of true educational equity. It calls on institutions not simply to accommodate disabled students, but to transform the conditions that have historically excluded them.

Understanding Ableism in Higher Education

Ableism in higher education is not limited to a lack of wheelchair ramps or the absence of captions on videos. It is a pervasive belief system that devalues disabled bodies and minds, defining them as deficient, disruptive, or disposable in academic spaces. This belief is embedded in institutional assumptions about what it means to be a "good" student: one who sits still, speaks fluently, meets deadlines, and thrives without support. These norms are neither neutral nor universal; they are constructed through white, neurotypical, middle-class values that marginalize anyone who does not conform. In this context, disability is not just under-supported, it is rendered incompatible with success. Postsecondary institutions, though committed to inclusion in rhetoric, often function as gatekeepers of access, opportunity, and legitimacy.

Ableism rarely stands alone. It intersects with racism, classism, sexism, heteronormativity, and linguistic discrimination to shape which students are perceived as competent, capable, or deserving. A Black student with a learning disability may be viewed as unmotivated rather than under-supported. A Latinx student who stutters may be dismissed as lacking professionalism rather than experiencing a communication disability. These biases affect not only how students are treated, but how they come to see themselves. When educators and administrators internalize these deficit narratives, they reinforce systems of exclusion under the guise of academic standards. Institutions must confront not only the material barriers facing disabled students but also the cultural ideologies that position disability as incompatible with academic excellence.

Perhaps most insidiously, ableism in higher education is often rationalized through appeals to rigor, tradition, or meritocracy. Professors may refuse to extend deadlines, ban the use of laptops, or penalize absences, citing fairness and standards rather than recognizing that such policies are inherently inequitable. Disability is framed as an exception to be managed, not as an identity to be respected or a perspective to be centered. The result is a campus culture in which disabled students are constantly asked to prove, perform, or suppress their needs to gain access to what others receive by default. Understanding ableism in higher education means recognizing that it is not an individual problem to be accommodated; it is a structural force to be dismantled.

The Burden of Accommodation

While accommodations are legally mandated under Section 504 of the Rehabilitation Act and the Americans with Disabilities Act (ADA), the way they are implemented in higher education often places the burden on students rather than institutions. Disabled students are expected to initiate, justify, and continually manage their access needs, navigating a bureaucratic process that can be dehumanizing, inconsistent, and retraumatizing. Rather than fostering inclusion, many accommodation systems function as barriers, reinforcing the idea that disability is an inconvenience rather than a diversity to be respected. This section explores two core aspects of this burden: the complexity of accessing accommodations and the personal cost of disclosing disability in academic spaces.

Navigating Bureaucracy and Inaccessibility

Accessing accommodations in college requires a level of bureaucratic navigation that many nondisabled peers never encounter. Students must gather documentation, meet with disability services offices, explain personal and often private information to strangers, and then negotiate accommodations with individual instructors, every semester, for every course. For students with multiple disabilities, intersecting identities, or unstable access to healthcare, this process can be especially daunting. As Snowden and Graaf (2019) note, systems built to support disabled people often reinforce dependency and control by prioritizing documentation over trust and access. Instead of assuming that students know what supports they need, institutions question their legitimacy, often demanding proof of "impairment" through outdated medical models.

This system also overlooks the lived realities of first-generation students, students from low-income households, and students of color. Many of these students lack the resources to pay for updated evaluations or navigate insurance systems that are hostile to mental health and developmental disability diagnoses (Artiga et al., 2020).

The result is a two-tiered system in which those with the financial and social capital to obtain documentation are more likely to access support, while others are left behind. Furthermore, some institutions only approve narrowly defined accommodations—extended time, note-takers, distraction-free rooms—without exploring broader supports like flexible attendance, alternative formats, or culturally responsive interventions. Bureaucratic inflexibility becomes another form of ableism, masking exclusion behind the appearance of compliance.

Disclosure, Stigma, and Emotional Labor

Requesting accommodations also requires students to disclose their disability status, often to people who are not trained in disability justice or trauma-informed care. Disclosure can be an emotionally taxing process, particularly for students with invisible or stigmatized disabilities such as learning disabilities, chronic illness, mental health conditions, or stuttering. Many students fear being judged, dismissed, or infantilized by faculty, and in too many cases, those fears are well-founded. Students report being told that accommodations are "unfair," being denied flexibility despite official documentation, or being publicly singled out in classrooms (Dolmage, 2017). The stress of disclosure and advocacy can take a toll on students' mental health and academic performance, not because of their disabilities, but because of how institutions respond to them.

For multiply marginalized students, disclosure is layered with additional risks. A student who is Black and autistic may hesitate to self-advocate in class, fearing that they will be perceived as aggressive or disruptive. A disabled immigrant student may worry that documentation requirements could conflict with their legal status or insurance coverage. These concerns are not hypothetical; they reflect real experiences of surveillance, criminalization, and neglect. Institutions often treat disclosure as a simple administrative task, ignoring the emotional labor and potential trauma involved. When access depends on disclosure, and disclosure is unsafe, the system fails.

To shift this burden, colleges and universities must rethink how accommodations are conceptualized and delivered. Instead of asking students to repeatedly request access, institutions must embed flexibility and accessibility into course design, policy, and campus life. Faculty should be trained not just in ADA compliance, but in disability as a social, cultural, and political identity. Accommodations should be offered proactively, with options available for students to opt in without needing to "prove" their needs. Ultimately, the responsibility to create accessible environments belongs to institutions, not the individuals seeking to survive within them.

Institutional Structures That Reinforce Exclusion

Although higher education institutions often express a commitment to diversity and inclusion, many of their internal structures continue to exclude disabled students through outdated pedagogies, rigid policies, and insufficient faculty preparation. These exclusions are rarely the result of overt discrimination. More often, they are embedded in the design of academic life itself, from course delivery and classroom layout to assessment models and faculty-student interactions. As a result, access becomes something that must be fought for rather than something that is guaranteed. This section examines how institutional norms and practices reinforce ableism, marginalize disabled students, and hinder meaningful participation. Table 7.1 illustrates key institutional barriers and offers justice-oriented responses that can shift higher education toward more inclusive, equity-driven practices.

Table 7.1 – Institutional Barriers and Justice-Oriented Solutions

Barrier	**Impact**	**Justice-Oriented Response**
Ableist Pedagogies	Excludes students through rigid teaching practices and inaccessible assessments.	Implement Universal Design for Learning (UDL) and inclusive pedagogy.
Punitive Academic Policies	Penalizes students for disability-related absences or delays, reinforcing inequity.	Revise policies to emphasize flexibility and student dignity.
Bureaucratic Accommodation Systems	Requires extensive documentation and self-disclosure, creating emotional burden.	Streamline accommodation processes and reduce proof burdens.

Barrier	Impact	Justice-Oriented Response
Faculty Inexperience With Disability	Leads to inconsistent support and potential discrimination in classrooms.	Mandate training on disability justice and inclusive practices.
Cultural Erasure of Disability	Contributes to invisibility and marginalization of disabled identities on campus.	Integrate disability into diversity initiatives and campus life.
Lack of Disabled Leadership	Limits institutional change and fails to reflect the diversity of the student body.	Develop leadership pipelines and mentorship programs for disabled individuals.

Inflexible Classroom Practices and Outdated Pedagogies

Traditional teaching methods continue to dominate postsecondary classrooms, privileging lecture-based instruction, timed assessments, and passive learning over inclusive, student-centered strategies. These formats assume that all students learn, process, and demonstrate knowledge in the same way and within the same time frame. For students with disabilities, especially those with learning, attention, or sensory differences, these assumptions create unnecessary barriers. A professor who prohibits laptops or requires oral participation without alternatives may unintentionally exclude students who rely on assistive technology or who experience anxiety and communication disabilities. Similarly, high-stakes testing formats and inflexible deadlines fail to account for fluctuating health conditions, neurodivergence, and processing variability.

Despite growing awareness of Universal Design for Learning (UDL), many institutions have not embedded these frameworks into faculty training or course design. As Dolmage (2017) argues, academic norms are steeped in ableism, often disguised as "rigor" or "tradition." The absence of flexibility in instructional practices sends a message: Disabled students must adapt to the system, not the other way around. This reinforces the idea that accessibility is a personal issue, not an institutional responsibility. To challenge this, colleges and universities must commit to redesigning pedagogy from the ground up, not as a retrofit, but as a foundation for equity.

Punitive and Rigid Academic Policies

Beyond the classroom, institutional policies often create additional structural obstacles. Attendance requirements, participation grades, and late work penalties are still common in many syllabi, regardless of student needs or accommodations. While intended to uphold academic standards, such policies disproportionately penalize students with chronic health issues, mental health conditions, or episodic disabilities. A student managing depression or recovering from surgery may be forced to choose between their health and their GPA. In many cases, requests for flexibility are met with suspicion, resistance, or bureaucratic delay, even when documentation is provided.

The problem is not simply individual policy decisions, but the broader institutional culture that prioritizes uniformity over access. Faculty are often granted wide discretion in applying policies, which can result in inconsistent responses to students with similar needs. This lack of standardization leaves students vulnerable to bias, misunderstanding, and inequity. For multiply marginalized students, such as disabled students of color or disabled LGBTQ+ students, these inconsistencies compound existing harms. Institutions must move away from punitive academic policies and adopt flexible frameworks that treat students with dignity and trust. Fairness is not about treating everyone the same, it's about ensuring that everyone has what they need to succeed.

Lack of Faculty Training and Accountability

Despite their critical role in ensuring access, most faculty members receive little to no training on disability, inclusive pedagogy, or legal obligations related to accommodations. This lack of preparation leaves instructors unaware of how their practices may be exclusionary and how to make meaningful changes. Some faculty may interpret disability accommodations as optional, burdensome, or incompatible with course objectives. Others may unintentionally perpetuate ableist language, ignore accessibility concerns in course materials, or conflate disability with academic unpreparedness. Without clear institutional expectations, these attitudes are rarely addressed, and disabled students are left to advocate for themselves in uneven and often harmful environments.

Accountability systems for accessibility are weak or nonexistent in most institutions. Course evaluations rarely include questions about accessibility, and departments are seldom evaluated on their inclusive teaching practices. Disability services offices are often underfunded and lack the authority to enforce faculty compliance, creating a culture where access is treated as peripheral rather than essential. This disconnect between disability services and academic affairs reflects a broader institutional failure to embed accessibility into the core of educational planning and evaluation. To shift this dynamic, institutions must make accessibility a shared, collective responsibility. Faculty must be evaluated and supported based on their ability to create inclusive learning environments, not just their publication records or student retention rates.

Institutions should also establish disability equity benchmarks across departments, link accessibility efforts to strategic plans, and provide financial incentives for faculty to redesign inaccessible courses. When inclusive teaching is viewed as pedagogically excellent, not as an accommodation, it elevates the entire learning experience. Accountability is not about punishment; it's about institutional integrity. Postsecondary institutions must move beyond statements of support and toward structures that guarantee access, affirm disabled identity, and eliminate ableist norms.

Campus Culture and Disability Erasure

Disability in higher education is not just a matter of physical access or legal compliance, it is a cultural issue. Across many campuses, disability remains largely invisible in diversity conversations, social spaces, and academic curricula. While institutions have made incremental progress in addressing race, gender, and sexuality, disability is frequently excluded from equity frameworks, or treated solely as a matter of individual accommodation. This erasure reinforces a campus culture in which disabled students are isolated, underrepresented, and misunderstood. Without active efforts to center disability as an identity and cultural experience, students are left to navigate hostile or indifferent environments that undermine their sense of belonging.

Lack of Disability Representation in Curriculum and Leadership

One of the most striking indicators of disability erasure is the absence of disability in course content, departmental priorities, and leadership structures. Few institutions offer courses on disability studies, and when they do, these courses are often siloed within special education departments rather than integrated across disciplines. Disability is not typically included in race, gender, or social justice frameworks in the humanities or social sciences and remains virtually absent in STEM fields. As Kerschbaum, Eisenman, and Jones (2017) argue, this absence signals that disability is not intellectually or politically relevant, despite its deep intersections with all facets of society.

In leadership, the pattern of exclusion continues. Disabled faculty, staff, and administrators are underrepresented at all levels of governance. Those who do disclose disability often face ableist attitudes about competence, productivity, or professionalism. When leadership does not reflect the diversity of its student body, it cannot fully respond to their needs or advocate for systemic change. Representation is not symbolic, it is structural. Campuses that lack disabled leadership will inevitably design policies and practices that overlook or harm disabled students. Institutions must actively recruit, retain, and uplift disabled leaders across academic and administrative roles to shift this narrative.

Social Isolation and Inaccessibility of Campus Life

Campus life often revolves around events, traditions, and activities that assume able-bodied participation. Club meetings in inaccessible spaces, student orientations packed with loud crowds and unstructured schedules, and residence halls with no elevator access all contribute to the marginalization of disabled students. Even when students are included on paper, they may experience subtle forms of exclusion, such as being "accommodated" in a way that separates them from peers or places them in a position of constant self-advocacy. These patterns of exclusion can lead to profound social isolation, which research shows has significant impacts on mental health, academic persistence, and overall well-being (Francis et al., 2019).

For many students with invisible disabilities, exclusion is also internalized. They may hide their needs to avoid stigma or push themselves past physical or emotional limits in an effort to fit in. Students who use mobility devices, use speech-generating tools, or have nonapparent disabilities often report feeling out of place, misunderstood, or hyper-visible in spaces that were never designed for them. When campus culture centers a narrow definition of "student life," it marginalizes anyone who cannot or does not conform. Institutions must recognize that inclusion is not just about academics, it is about creating a community where all students are seen, valued, and supported in every aspect of campus life.

Maintaining the Status Quo Through Silence

The most insidious form of disability erasure is silence. Silence in classroom discussions, where disability is never named as a site of oppression. Silence in hiring committees, where accommodations are feared rather than normalized. Silence in diversity statements, where disability is either omitted or reduced to a footnote. This silence allows ableism to operate unchallenged, rendering it invisible and therefore unaccountable. When institutions fail to name and confront ableism, they normalize exclusion.

As Dolmage (2017) explains, ableism thrives in the rhetorical practices of the academy, its syllabi, mission statements, and institutional priorities. It is not enough for campuses to be physically accessible; they must also be rhetorically accessible, naming disability as a valued identity and source of cultural knowledge. When disability is included only in response to complaints or crises, it remains peripheral and conditional. To shift culture, institutions must center disability as integral to educational excellence and justice. Naming is the first step toward accountability.

Toward Disability Justice in Postsecondary Education

Disability justice in higher education requires more than accessibility, it requires transformation. While disability services offices play a vital role in ensuring individual accommodations, they cannot dismantle the structural inequities embedded in academic culture, policy, and design. To advance true equity, institutions must move beyond a compliance mindset and reimagine the way they define success, build community, and design learning. This means centering disabled people, not as problems to be solved but as leaders, knowledge-holders, and co-creators of institutional change. The following subsections explore key strategies for embedding disability justice into the fabric of postsecondary institutions: UDL, the creation of disability cultural centers, and leadership pathways for disabled students and faculty.

Universal Design for Learning and Inclusive Pedagogy

UDL is a research-based framework that offers flexible approaches to teaching and learning, allowing students multiple means of engagement, representation, and expression. Rather than retrofitting classrooms after students request accommodations, UDL anticipates variability and proactively removes barriers to learning. It shifts the question from "How do I accommodate this student?" to "How do I design my course so all students can access it from the start?" This mindset reframes access as a matter of quality, not exception, and benefits all learners, not just those with disabilities.

Implementing UDL requires a fundamental shift in faculty mindset, training, and practice. It means rethinking assessment (e.g., offering alternatives to timed exams), reimagining participation (e.g., valuing multiple forms of communication), and redesigning course materials (e.g., captioned videos, screen reader–friendly documents). Faculty must also adopt a posture of humility and openness, recognizing that academic excellence includes accessibility, rather than being achieved in spite of it. Institutions can support this shift by integrating UDL into faculty development programs, requiring inclusive course design in evaluation criteria and incentivizing accessibility innovation through funding and recognition.

Importantly, UDL must be implemented with attention to intersectionality. For students who are multilingual, undocumented, low income, or otherwise marginalized, access is shaped by more than cognitive difference, it is shaped by racism, classism, and cultural bias. Inclusive pedagogy must reflect this complexity, engaging with multiple ways of knowing and resisting a narrow definition of academic success. UDL is not a checklist; it is a philosophy of justice and respect. When institutions commit to this model, they send a powerful message: Disabled students are not burdens, they are scholars, creators, and members of the academic community.

Disability Cultural Centers and Affirming Spaces

Disability cultural centers are physical and symbolic spaces where disabled students can gather, build community, and explore disability as an identity, not just a diagnosis. These centers function much like multicultural centers or LGBTQ+ resource centers: They provide programming, peer support, advocacy training, and cultural affirmation. They challenge the medicalized approach to disability found in most disability services offices and instead frame disability as a source of pride, resistance, and political consciousness. For many students, particularly those with intersecting marginalized identities, these spaces are critical for survival and empowerment.

Despite their importance, disability cultural centers are still rare on college campuses. Most institutions provide legal accommodations but fail to invest in the relational and cultural dimensions of disability inclusion. As a result, students often lack spaces to connect with others who share their experiences and values. The absence of such spaces contributes to ongoing erasure, as discussed in the previous section. Institutions must recognize that access is not only legal, it is emotional, cultural, and collective. Creating and sustaining disability cultural centers requires institutional commitment, funding, and leadership by disabled people themselves.

These centers also serve a broader educational function. They can host guest speakers, organize cross-campus teach-ins, build coalitions with other identity groups, and curate exhibitions of disability art, history, and activism. They create pathways for students to move from isolation to leadership, from marginalization to visibility. When supported properly, disability cultural centers can catalyze campus-wide change and shift the narrative around what inclusion truly means. Postsecondary institutions that are serious about equity must build structures that not only accommodate disabled students, but affirm, celebrate, and empower them.

Leadership Pipelines and Institutional Accountability

Creating access to leadership opportunities for disabled students, staff, and faculty is essential to transforming higher education. Without representation in decision-making spaces, curriculum committees, tenure review boards, student government, and presidential advisory councils, disability will remain peripheral to institutional priorities. Leadership pipelines must begin early, with intentional mentorship, peer networking, and funded fellowships that affirm disabled students' potential. Institutions should also examine their own internal policies: Are hiring practices inclusive? Are leadership roles accessible? Are disabled voices centered in conversations about diversity, equity, and inclusion?

Disabled faculty often face systemic barriers to promotion and tenure, including biased student evaluations, inflexible teaching expectations, and tokenization in service roles. These barriers must be identified and dismantled through equity audits, inclusive evaluation criteria, and protected time for disability-related research and service. For staff and administrators, opportunities for advancement must be clearly communicated, and accommodations for leadership roles must be normalized, not stigmatized. Accountability requires transparency; institutions should collect and publish disaggregated data on leadership demographics and retention, ensuring that progress is measurable and visible.

Most importantly, leadership pipelines must be rooted in a disability justice ethos. Leadership should not be about assimilating into ableist structures but transforming them. Disabled leaders bring lived experience, creativity, and vision that are essential to building inclusive and equitable institutions. Their presence disrupts dominant narratives about who is qualified to lead, teach, and shape the future of education. When campuses cultivate and support disabled leadership at all levels, they move from symbolic inclusion to structural transformation.

Conclusion

Addressing ableism in postsecondary education requires more than programmatic fixes, it demands a cultural, structural, and ideological transformation. The systems that were not built with disabled students in mind continue to reproduce exclusion unless institutions are willing to interrogate and dismantle the norms they uphold. From inaccessible pedagogy to harmful disclosure practices, from the invisibility of disability in campus life to the absence of disabled leadership, the barriers are numerous, but they are not insurmountable. Disability justice calls on institutions to move from intent to impact, from rhetoric to accountability, and from accommodation to true inclusion.

This chapter has argued that disability must be centered in every conversation about equity and excellence in higher education. It must be named, resourced, and led by those who live its complexities. Transforming institutions to meet the needs of all students means challenging long-standing ideas about merit, participation, and academic worthiness. But it also opens the door to new forms of community, knowledge, and possibility—forms that benefit everyone, not just those who have been historically excluded.

As we look ahead to the next chapter, I turn to the role that technology can play in supporting or undermining these efforts. While digital tools offer unprecedented opportunities for access and innovation, they also risk reinforcing exclusion if not designed and implemented equitably. Chapter 8 explores how technology, when grounded in justice and designed with disabled users at the center, can become a powerful force in advancing postsecondary success.

References

Artiga, S., Orgera, K., & Pham, O. (2020). *Disparities in health and health care: Five key questions and answers*. Kaiser Family Foundation. https://www.kff.org

Dolmage, J. T. (2017). *Academic ableism: Disability and higher education*. University of Michigan Press.

Francis, G. L., Duke, J. M., Fujita, M., & Sutton, J. C. (2019). "It's a constant fight:" Experiences of college students with disabilities. *Journal of Postsecondary Education and Disability*, *32*(3), 247–262.

Kerschbaum, S. L., Eisenman, L. T., & Jones, R. M. (2017). *Negotiating disability: Disclosure and higher education*. University of Michigan Press.

Snowden, L., & Graaf, G. (2019). The "undeserving poor," racial bias, and Medicaid coverage of African Americans. *Journal of Black Psychology*, *45*(3), 130–142.

CHAPTER 8

The Role of Technology in Enhancing Postsecondary Success

Technology is increasingly central to the postsecondary experience. From digital course platforms to adaptive software, it shapes how students access content, communicate with instructors, and navigate campus systems. For students with disabilities, technology can be a powerful tool to enhance independence, learning, and community participation. As discussed in Chapter 6, students preparing for adult life require flexible supports that foster autonomy and interdependence. Similarly, as highlighted in Chapter 7, institutional ableism often shows up in the form of inflexible teaching practices and inaccessible systems. Technology, when intentionally designed and equitably implemented, can help bridge these gaps by offering tools that adapt to diverse learning needs, reduce unnecessary barriers, and affirm student agency.

Yet the promise of technology is not inherently just. Without careful attention, digital tools can replicate the very exclusions they aim to address. Platforms that are not screen-reader-friendly, captioning software that misrepresents speech, or proctoring systems that penalize neurodivergent behaviors are examples of how innovation can reinforce ableism. This chapter explores how colleges and universities can move beyond a transactional view of technology to embrace it as a means of liberation. It calls on institutions to critically examine the digital landscape and to co-design technological solutions with, not just for, disabled students.

Building from the foundation laid in earlier chapters, this discussion will explore how technology intersects with accessibility, cultural relevance, instructional design, and student empowerment. Rather than viewing technology as an add-on or afterthought, this chapter centers it as a key pillar in realizing the full vision of postsecondary equity for disabled students.

Assistive Technology in Higher Education

Assistive technology plays a critical role in supporting students with disabilities in higher education. These tools, which include screen readers, speech-to-text software, alternative input devices, captioning platforms, and augmentative and alternative communication (AAC) tools, are designed to provide access to content, facilitate communication, and support executive functioning and organization. When implemented equitably, assistive technology empowers students to learn and engage in ways that reflect their strengths and needs. It reduces dependence on others and affirms students' right to participate fully in academic life. For many students, these tools serve as a gateway to autonomy and confidence in navigating postsecondary environments (Al-Azawei et al., 2016; Edyburn, 2013).

Despite its promise, access to assistive technology remains inconsistent. Students may not know what supports are available or may be unsure of how to request them. Financial barriers often prevent students from purchasing the devices or software they need. Disability services offices, while essential, may be under-resourced and lack the staffing or capacity to provide in-depth training on how to use technology effectively (Madaus, 2011). In some cases, institutions limit access to technology by requiring extensive medical documentation or offering supports only to students who meet rigid eligibility criteria. These barriers shift the responsibility for access from the institution to the individual, creating additional labor for students already navigating complex academic and social systems (Friedman & VanPuymbrouck, 2019).

The value of assistive technology is undermined when classroom practices and institutional systems do not support its use. A screen reader cannot provide access to scanned PDFs if instructors fail to upload accessible versions of course materials. Dictation software becomes ineffective if participation is graded only through written responses or in-class discussions. These examples reveal a misalignment between the design of educational systems and the technological supports that enable students to succeed. Without coordinated support from faculty, instructional designers, and campus leadership, assistive technology remains underutilized or misunderstood (Dickey, 2022). Institutions must prioritize accessibility as a shared responsibility, not a specialized add-on.

Using assistive technology is not simply a matter of functionality. It is also deeply tied to students' sense of self, belonging, and empowerment. Students who are encouraged to explore and use assistive tools report greater academic engagement and self-efficacy. In contrast, when the use of technology is stigmatized, viewed as evidence of deficiency rather than difference, students may choose not to use the supports they need. Creating a campus culture where assistive technology is normalized and affirmed is essential. This includes modeling its use in faculty practices, providing peer mentorship opportunities, and incorporating technology into campus-wide inclusion strategies (Kerschbaum et al., 2017).

Assistive technology should be understood as part of a larger ecosystem of support, not a standalone solution. While it can provide vital access, it does not eliminate the need for inclusive policies, accessible instructional practices, and community-based support. Autonomy is strengthened when students are given not only the tools they need, but the freedom to use them without fear of judgment or penalty. When institutions embrace assistive technology as a core component of equity and learning design, they move closer to creating environments where all students can thrive.

Inclusive Instructional Design and Universal Access

Technology alone cannot close access gaps in higher education; it must be coupled with intentional, inclusive instructional design. As institutions increasingly adopt digital platforms to deliver content, assess learning, and manage classrooms, it is imperative that these systems are built and used with accessibility at their core. When digital tools are designed for a narrow definition of the "typical" student, they often exclude learners whose needs diverge from dominant academic norms. Inclusive instructional design acknowledges the full diversity of student experiences and ensures that technology works not only functionally, but equitably. The following subsections explore how learning management systems, the Universal Design for Learning (UDL) framework, and instructional flexibility can collectively shape more accessible postsecondary environments.

Designing Learning Management Systems for Accessibility

Learning management systems (LMSs) such as Canvas, Blackboard, and Moodle have become central to the delivery of instruction in higher education. These platforms serve as digital classrooms, providing access to syllabi, assignments, readings, discussion boards, and grades. However, many LMSs are not fully accessible by default. For students who use screen readers, keyboard navigation, or alternative input devices, accessing core course content can be unnecessarily complex. Issues such as unlabeled buttons, inconsistent navigation, or inaccessible PDF uploads create daily challenges that prevent students from participating on equal footing.

Institutional responsibility extends beyond choosing a compliant LMS; it includes ensuring that faculty know how to use the platform in ways that preserve accessibility. Even when the LMS itself meets accessibility standards, instructors may unknowingly upload inaccessible documents, link to uncaptioned videos, or use embedded tools that are not compatible with assistive technology. Faculty training is therefore essential. Universities must invest in onboarding processes, accessibility toolkits, and support staff who can help instructors design courses that meet diverse learner needs. When LMSs are used as inclusive hubs rather than static bulletin boards, they can foster engagement, clarity, and autonomy for all students.

Applying Universal Design for Learning in Digital Spaces

UDL is a framework for instructional design that promotes flexibility and anticipates learner variability. Rather than providing a single path for engagement, representation, and expression, UDL encourages multiple modes of participation so that students can learn in ways that align with their strengths. In digital classrooms, UDL is particularly powerful. Instructors can embed captions in videos, provide transcripts and audio versions of lectures, use visual and textual materials, and offer varied assignment formats such as podcasts, infographics, or written responses. These strategies benefit not only students with disabilities, but English language learners, working students, and those with different cognitive styles.

However, UDL is not self-executing. It requires a philosophical commitment to equity and the design time to implement meaningful options. Faculty may hesitate to adopt UDL principles due to time constraints, misconceptions about rigor, or lack of institutional incentives. Institutions can address these challenges by embedding UDL into teaching evaluation processes, encouraging innovation through professional development, and highlighting examples of inclusive practice across departments. Importantly, UDL is not about lowering expectations—it is about raising opportunity. When students are given multiple avenues to succeed, they are more likely to persist, retain knowledge, and contribute meaningfully to the learning environment.

Instructional Flexibility as an Equity Practice

Rigid academic policies are often framed as necessary for maintaining high standards. Yet these inflexible rules, such as mandatory attendance, fixed deadlines, or one-size-fits-all assessments, can create serious barriers for students with disabilities. Instructional flexibility is not the same as leniency; it is an intentional practice rooted in the understanding that students' lives are complex, unpredictable, and shaped by more than what happens inside the classroom. Building flexibility into course design means offering grace without requiring crisis. It means allowing extensions when needed, providing asynchronous options when possible, and assessing learning through varied, meaningful tasks.

Instructors may worry that flexibility leads to inconsistency or lowers expectations. These concerns can be addressed through transparent syllabus design, clear communication, and structured choices. Providing a menu of assignment formats, for instance, gives students control over how they demonstrate knowledge while still aligning with learning objectives. Using a "drop-the-lowest-grade" policy or allowing participation through multiple modalities also helps students remain engaged even during challenging times. Flexibility communicates trust in students' ability to manage their learning and affirms that success is not measured by uniformity, but by growth.

Inclusive instructional design does not replace the need for structural accessibility, it enhances it. When learning platforms are built for usability, courses are designed with variability in mind, and flexibility is viewed as a standard practice, higher education begins to shift from accommodation to inclusion. Still, as institutions increasingly rely on digital tools, new challenges arise around surveillance, bias, and data ethics. The next section explores these tensions by examining how certain technologies, especially those used to monitor or evaluate students, may reinforce ableism rather than reduce it.

Surveillance, Privacy, and Digital Ableism

While technology in higher education can expand access, it can also reproduce ableism in more insidious forms. Surveillance tools, such as remote proctoring software, classroom monitoring systems, and behavioral analytics platforms, are increasingly embedded into digital learning environments under the guise of accountability and academic integrity. Yet these systems are rarely designed with disabled users in mind. Their rigid assumptions about how students behave, communicate, and learn often clash with the realities of neurodivergent, chronically ill, or physically disabled students. When institutions adopt surveillance technologies without regard for privacy, equity, or accessibility, they risk causing harm to the very students they claim to support.

Remote Proctoring and Neurodivergent Harms

Remote proctoring software such as ProctorU, Respondus, and Honorlock has become widespread in postsecondary settings. These platforms use facial recognition, gaze detection, noise monitoring, and screen recording to flag what they label as suspicious behavior. For neurodivergent students, these systems can be especially discriminatory. A student with ADHD may fidget or look away from the screen, triggering a red flag. A student with autism may struggle to make sustained eye contact. A student who stutters may hesitate or repeat themselves when speaking into a microphone. These behaviors are misinterpreted by algorithmic systems that have been trained on normative patterns of behavior, often rooted in able-bodied assumptions (Gillis & Spiess, 2019; Lupton, 2020).

Furthermore, the stress of being surveilled, especially in high-stakes testing environments, can trigger anxiety, trauma responses, and executive functioning challenges. Students have reported avoiding accommodations altogether to sidestep additional scrutiny. Others have shared experiences of proctoring software failing to recognize their faces due to lighting issues, skin tone, or facial differences, which results in test interruptions or disqualification. The consequences are academic penalties and psychological harm, both of which disproportionately affect disabled and marginalized students. Proctoring tools, when not thoughtfully implemented or regulated, reinforce ableist notions of what a "good student" looks like and pathologize natural variation in human behavior.

Data Collection, Consent, and Power

Surveillance in higher education extends beyond exams. Learning analytics platforms track students' log-in times, click patterns, page views, and discussion participation. Biometric attendance scanners verify classroom presence. Campus safety apps track students' movements. While these systems are often marketed as tools for improving outcomes or protecting student well-being, they also raise serious concerns about privacy, consent, and data exploitation (PEN America, 2022). Students are rarely given meaningful opportunities to opt out or to understand how their data will be used, stored, or shared.

Disabled students are particularly vulnerable in these data ecosystems. Information about accommodations, mental health, medication usage, or disability status may be indirectly revealed through system interactions or flagged patterns. When institutions fail to safeguard this information or disclose how it's used, they create environments of mistrust and risk retraumatizing students who already navigate stigmatization. The power imbalance between institutions and students, especially for those dependent on services or financial aid, means that many students feel pressured to accept invasive policies without objection. In this context, data collection becomes a tool of control rather than support.

Ethical technology use in higher education must prioritize informed consent, limit unnecessary surveillance, and ensure transparency in data collection. Institutions must publicly disclose how surveillance tools are evaluated for bias, how student data is protected, and how students can seek recourse when harm occurs. Faculty, IT departments, and disability services must work together to ensure that the pursuit of "efficiency" does not come at the expense of student dignity or rights. Data should inform access, not discipline difference.

Algorithmic Bias and Systemic Exclusion

Many digital platforms in education rely on artificial intelligence and algorithmic decision-making. These algorithms determine risk scores, flag disengagement, recommend interventions, or adjust learning paths. However, algorithms are not neutral, they reflect the values and biases of those who design them. If datasets used to train these systems exclude or underrepresent disabled people, the resulting models will reproduce systemic exclusion (Benjamin, 2019; Noble, 2018). For example, predictive analytics may label a student who requests frequent extensions or misses log-ins due to chronic illness as "at risk," triggering unnecessary interventions or assumptions about capability.

Algorithmic bias also impacts disabled students of color at the intersection of racism and ableism. Systems designed without attention to racialized disability experiences often misinterpret behaviors or overlook context. As a result, interventions may be punitive rather than supportive. A Black student with ADHD may be flagged for low engagement, while a white neurotypical student exhibiting similar patterns is perceived as independent. These misclassifications reveal how automated systems often amplify the very inequities they aim to address. Without careful auditing, inclusive design practices, and cross-disciplinary collaboration, educational technology risks becoming a digital extension of structural discrimination.

Institutions must actively interrogate the algorithms they use and demand transparency from vendors about model design, training data, and impact evaluations. Disabled students and advocates should be involved in these conversations from the start, not as afterthoughts, but as co-creators. Disability justice requires moving beyond compliance with accessibility checklists to dismantling the systems that create and normalize technological harm. When technology is designed through the lens of equity and implemented with integrity, it can support, not surveil, disabled students in postsecondary education.

Digital Literacy and Equity Gaps

Technology plays a crucial role in enabling access to higher education, yet disparities in digital access and fluency remain persistent and deeply inequitable. For students with disabilities, particularly those from low-income, rural, and racially marginalized communities, the digital divide presents real barriers to participation and success. These inequities go beyond devices and Wi-Fi; they reflect broader structural inequalities in education systems, public infrastructure, and institutional priorities (Auxier & Anderson, 2020; Robinson et al., 2015). Addressing digital literacy and access is not just about integrating new technologies but about transforming how institutions serve students who have historically been excluded from full participation in academic life.

The Digital Divide and Infrastructural Disparities

Many postsecondary institutions assume a baseline level of digital access and device ownership, yet the reality is far more uneven. Students without broadband internet or updated technology cannot consistently access online course content, complete assignments, or engage in hybrid learning environments. For disabled students who rely on assistive technologies, such as screen readers, dictation software, or AAC devices, this lack of access is compounded by the need for specialized equipment that is often expensive or unsupported by campus IT systems (Office of Educational Technology, 2022).

Research during the COVID-19 pandemic exposed the scope of the problem. Pew data found that 59% of low-income parents reported their child may face digital barriers to schoolwork, including unreliable internet or lack of devices (Auxier & Anderson, 2020). Students with disabilities were also more likely to experience disruption, as remote learning platforms were rarely designed with accessibility in mind (Ngwacho, 2020). While emergency measures such as laptop loans and Wi-Fi hotspots were implemented in some districts, they were temporary and unevenly distributed. Long-term solutions require deeper investment in both physical infrastructure and inclusive planning.

Access is not just about physical connectivity, it also involves whether students can use the tools effectively. Devices must be compatible with assistive technologies, and digital environments must be designed for navigation by all users. Institutions must ensure their platforms meet accessibility standards and that students have access to the training, support, and tools needed to use them with confidence and autonomy.

Digital Literacy as a Civil Rights Imperative

Digital literacy refers to the ability to effectively find, evaluate, use, and create information using digital technologies. For disabled students, digital literacy includes the ability to navigate assistive tools, protect privacy in digital spaces, and advocate for accessible design in educational and employment settings. These skills are critical for success in postsecondary education, yet many students are expected to arrive at college already proficient in them, a problematic assumption given the unequal quality of K-12 digital instruction (Bailey & Nyabola, 2021).

Students from under-resourced schools may have had little or no exposure to screen readers, alternative input devices, or voice-to-text technology. Some may have been actively discouraged from using technology that could support them, due to ableist beliefs or outdated infrastructure. Others may have received training on outdated tools that no longer align with college-level requirements. These disparities compound at the postsecondary level, where students are often expected to self-advocate and self-navigate complex digital systems with minimal guidance.

Institutions must treat digital literacy as a foundational right, not an optional enhancement. Offering credit-bearing digital literacy courses, integrated support services, and hands-on workshops helps bridge these gaps. Faculty also play a key role in modeling accessible digital practices and in understanding when lack of engagement may reflect lack of access, rather than lack of motivation. Elevating digital literacy is not only about supporting students' academic goals, it is about affirming their right to participate fully in the digital society.

Institutional Responsibility and Inclusive Tech Support

Institutions have a duty to ensure that all students can access and meaningfully engage with digital resources. This begins with internal audits of who has access to what technology and support. Disaggregated data should be collected across lines of race, income, disability status, and geography to reveal patterns in student experience. These insights must be used to inform responsive strategies, including providing subsidized devices, universal software access, and robust onboarding for new students (Office of Educational Technology, 2022).

Technology support services also need to evolve. IT teams must be trained in assistive technology and digital accessibility, and students must have access to support staff who can answer questions without judgment or delay. Multiple access points, including virtual, in-person, and mobile options, ensure that students aren't excluded due to physical location or time constraints. Institutions should also create public-private partnerships to extend access beyond campus, including collaborations with local libraries and broadband providers.

Digital equity must be integrated into strategic planning, not relegated to short-term initiatives. Institutions that treat access as a justice issue, rather than a budgetary afterthought, position themselves to serve the full spectrum of learners and to meet the demands of a changing educational landscape.

The Role of Public Policy in Digital Equity

While colleges and universities must lead in digital inclusion, lasting change also depends on public policy. Government programs like the Emergency Connectivity Fund and the Affordable Connectivity Program have helped expand broadband access for eligible families, but much more is needed to support postsecondary students with disabilities (U.S. Department of Education, 2017). Policy must prioritize infrastructure investment in underserved communities and fund the purchase and support of assistive technology as a basic educational right.

Grants and funding formulas should include accessibility mandates and equity benchmarks. Policymakers should also require public reporting on digital access gaps and create incentives for institutions to close them. At the federal level, updates to laws such as the Higher Education Act and the Americans with Disabilities Act could mandate stronger digital accessibility standards and provide enforcement mechanisms for noncompliance.

Higher education leaders can play a critical role by advocating for these reforms. As institutions increasingly rely on digital platforms, they must push for policies that ensure those platforms are equitable, accessible, and accountable. Without coordinated public action, digital exclusion will remain a structural barrier to educational justice.

Transparency, Data, and Accountability

Institutional accountability is essential to eliminating digital inequities. Disaggregated data collection on access to devices, digital literacy outcomes, and usage of assistive technology must be standardized and made publicly available. Transparency allows stakeholders, students, families, faculty, and policymakers to understand who is being served and who is being left behind (Robinson et al., 2015).

Procurement policies must also reflect institutional values. When campuses adopt new platforms or proctoring tools, they must require vendors to provide accessibility documentation, inclusive design plans, and ethical data use policies. Technology should not be selected solely for cost or popularity; it must align with the institution's commitment to universal design and student well-being. Vendor contracts should include clear accountability structures, including pathways for student feedback and remediation of access violations. Building digital equity into the foundation of higher education is both possible and necessary. It requires a commitment to transparency, student voice, and systemic accountability. When technology is deployed with equity as its guiding principle, it becomes not only a tool for access, but a catalyst for justice. Table 8.1 presents common technological barriers alongside equity-centered strategies that institutions can adopt to ensure accessible and inclusive digital learning environments.

Table 8.1 – Technological Barriers and Equity-Centered Solutions in Postsecondary Education

Barrier	Impacted Groups	Equity-Centered Solutions
Inaccessible learning platforms (e.g., Learning Management Systems issues)	Students using screen readers, alternative inputs	Mandatory accessible course design training for faculty; accessibility audits
Limited access to assistive technology	Low-income students, rural students	Institutional funding for tech loans; peer mentoring for tool training
Surveillance-based tools that penalize neurodivergence	Neurodivergent, chronically ill, and racialized students	Replace proctoring with inclusive assessments; involve students in policy review
Algorithmic bias in learning analytics	Disabled students of color	Transparent audits of AI tools; co-design committees including disabled students
Digital literacy disparities	Students from underfunded K-12 backgrounds	Credit-bearing courses on digital tools; embedded tech coaching in advising
Poor integration of Universal Design for Learning in digital instruction	All students with diverse learning needs	Universal Design for Learning embedded in all instructional design and evaluation processes
Inconsistent tech support for assistive tech use	Students with complex disabilities	Cross-training IT and disability staff; multiple tech support formats
Data privacy and consent violations	All marginalized students	Clear opt-out policies; student-centered consent forms; data use transparency requirements

Student-Centered Innovation—Co-Design and Empowerment

Technology in postsecondary education should not be developed or implemented without the full participation of students, especially those with disabilities. When digital tools are created or adopted without their input, they often reflect institutional biases and reinforce ableist assumptions about how students should learn, communicate, or engage. Disabled students are not passive recipients of technology, they are experts in navigating and resisting inaccessible systems, and they hold valuable insights that should guide innovation. Centering these students in the design and decision-making process moves institutions from a model of charity or compliance to one of collaboration and equity. Student-centered innovation honors the lived expertise of disabled students and views their participation as critical to creating truly inclusive digital environments (Office of Educational Technology, 2022).

The Power of Co-Design in Inclusive Innovation

Co-design refers to an intentional, collaborative process where users and developers work together to shape solutions. In higher education, this means engaging disabled students from the earliest stages of technology development: not merely asking them to test a nearly finished product, but inviting them to define problems, suggest priorities, and evaluate outcomes. Students bring diverse perspectives that challenge dominant assumptions about access and usability, helping to identify barriers that developers and administrators might overlook. Their feedback can lead to more responsive, relevant, and empowering technologies that reflect real-world needs and contexts (Robinson et al., 2015). Institutions that create structured opportunities for co-design, such as digital access advisory boards, participatory research initiatives, or inclusive innovation hubs, demonstrate a commitment to shared power and student agency.

Reframing Technology as a Tool for Collective Empowerment

Technology is often framed narrowly as a means of increasing productivity, efficiency, or academic performance. But for disabled students, it can also serve as a tool for connection, community-building, and advocacy. When students use digital tools to design accessible course materials, teach others how to use assistive software, or organize for institutional change, they are practicing a form of innovation that is grounded in justice. These actions demonstrate how disabled students are not only consumers of technology, but creators and leaders within the digital landscape. Institutions can support this work by funding student-led accessibility projects, recognizing digital advocacy in academic awards, and integrating accessibility centers into broader campus technology strategies (Bailey & Nyabola, 2021).

Sustaining a Culture of Student-Centered Technology

Creating more equitable digital environments is not a one-time initiative, it requires sustained investment in culture change. Institutions must build ongoing mechanisms for students to provide feedback on the accessibility and functionality of technology across campus. These mechanisms should be transparent, responsive, and led by teams that include students with disabilities as decision-makers. When students see that their input is valued and leads to change, they are more likely to stay engaged and to trust the institution's commitment to inclusion (Office of Educational Technology, 2022). Faculty and staff also need to be trained in co-design principles so they can facilitate meaningful collaboration with students and model inclusive practices in their own teaching and service.

Structural Commitments to Student Voice and Access

Institutions that claim to prioritize equity must embed student voice into their governance and planning structures. This includes appointing disabled students to campus technology committees, establishing accountability metrics for accessibility innovation, and ensuring that funding is allocated to projects that reflect student-defined needs. Faculty evaluations and administrative reviews should include criteria for inclusive technology use and responsiveness to student feedback. These structural commitments move beyond performative inclusion and help to redistribute power within the university. When disabled students are seen as co-creators rather than accommodation-seekers, technology becomes a site of possibility and transformation, not just compliance.

Student-centered innovation asks institutions to redefine who holds knowledge and who shapes the learning environment. It rejects the idea that educational technology must be developed top-down and instead imagines a future in which access is co-created and justice is nonnegotiable. By investing in student-led solutions and recognizing the leadership of disabled students, colleges and universities can build digital systems that reflect their highest values. Technology, when guided by the people it is meant to serve, becomes not just a bridge to access but a foundation for liberation.

Conclusion

Technology holds transformative potential for students with disabilities, but only when it is designed, implemented, and maintained with equity and justice at the center. Throughout this chapter, we have explored the promises and perils of digital innovation in higher education. From inclusive instructional design to the dangers of surveillance, from gaps in digital literacy to the power of co-design, one truth remains consistent: Access alone is not enough. The true measure of technological equity lies in whether students with disabilities feel seen, respected, and empowered, not just accommodated.

Institutions must move beyond reactive accommodations and begin cultivating ecosystems that anticipate difference, that normalize variation in learning and communication, and that position disabled students not as problems to solve, but as leaders to follow. Equity in digital environments is not simply a technical issue; it is a reflection of institutional values, priorities, and courage. When disabled students are invited to co-create these systems, the result is not just better tools, it is a better educational experience for all.

As we move into Chapter 9, we shift from frameworks and practices to the heart of the matter: lived experience. In the next chapter, we will hear directly from students with disabilities as they reflect on their postsecondary journeys, challenges, and triumphs. These narratives ground the theory in reality and remind us why this work matters. Their stories are not anecdotes, they are evidence. And they demand that we listen, learn, and act accordingly.

References

Al-Azawei, A., Serenelli, F., & Lundqvist, K. (2016). Universal Design for Learning (UDL): A content analysis of peer reviewed journals from 2012 to 2015. *Journal of the Scholarship of Teaching and Learning, 16*(3), 39–56.

Auxier, B., & Anderson, M. (2020). *As schools close due to the coronavirus, some U.S. students face a digital 'homework gap'*. Pew Research Center. https://www.pewresearch.org/internet/2020/03/16/as-schools-close-due-to-the-coronavirus-some-u-s-students-face-a-digital-homework-gap/

Bailey, L. E., & Nyabola, N. (2021). Digital equity as an enabling platform for equality and inclusion. *Pathfinders for Peaceful, Just, and Inclusive Societies/NYU Center on International Cooperation, June 2021.* https://cic.nyu.edu/resources/digital-equity-as-an-enabling-platform-for-equality-and-inclusion

Benjamin, R. (2019). *Race after technology: Abolitionist tools for the new Jim Code.* Polity Press.

Dickey, D. D. (2022). *Exploring students with disabilities' experiences and perceptions of assistive technology use in a postsecondary education environment: A concurrent transformative mixed methods study.* Drexel University.

Dolmage, J. T. (2017). *Academic ableism: Disability and higher education.* University of Michigan Press.

Edyburn, D. L. (2013). Critical issues in advancing the special education technology evidence base. *Exceptional Children, 80*(1), 7–24.

Friedman, C., & VanPuymbrouck, L. (2019). The relationship between disability prejudice and Medicaid home and community-based services spending. *Disability and Health Journal, 12*(3), 359–365.

Gillis, T. B., & Spiess, J. L. (2019). Big data and discrimination. *The University of Chicago Law Review, 86*(2), 459-488.

Kerschbaum, S. L., Eisenman, L. T., & Jones, R. M. (2017). *Negotiating disability: Disclosure and higher education.* University of Michigan Press.

Lupton, D. (2020). *Data selves: More-than-human perspectives.* Polity Press.

Madaus, J. W. (2011). The history of disability services in higher education. *New Directions for Higher Education, 154,* 5–15.

Ngwacho, A. G. (2020). COVID-19 pandemic impact on Kenyan education sector: Learner challenges and mitigations. *Journal of Research Innovation and Implications in Education, 4*(2), 128–139.

Noble, S. U. (2018). *Algorithms of oppression: How search engines reinforce racism.* NYU Press.

Office of Educational Technology, U.S. Department of Education. (2022). *Advancing digital equity for all: U.S. Department of Education digital equity education roundtables.* https://tech.ed.gov/files/2022/09/DEER-Report-9-2022.pdf

PEN America. (2022). *Educational surveillance: The dangers of monitoring students' online activity.* https://pen.org/educational-surveillance

Robinson, L., Cotten, S. R., Ono, H., Quan-Haase, A., Mesch, G., Chen, W., Schulz, J., Hale, T. M., & Stern, M. J. (2015). Digital inequalities and why they matter. *Information, Communication & Society, 18*(5), 569–582. https://doi.org/10.1080/1369118X.2015.1012532

U.S. Department of Education. (2017). *Reimagining the role of technology in education: 2017 National Education Technology Plan Update.* https://tech.ed.gov/files/2017/01/NETP17.pdf

CHAPTER 9

Voices of Lived Experience

Why Lived Experience Matters

In the study of postsecondary education, data often takes the form of spreadsheets, surveys, and institutional metrics. Graduation rates, retention trends, and accommodation usage are routinely analyzed to measure student success. But numbers alone cannot capture the complexity of what it means to navigate college as a disabled person. Behind every data point is a story, of struggle, resilience, exclusion, and hope. In this chapter, we turn our attention to those stories. Not as supplemental to the research, but as evidence in their own right.

Lived experience is not anecdotal, it is empirical. It is rooted in the daily navigation of barriers and the emotional labor of confronting ableism embedded within policies, pedagogy, and campus culture. The voices of disabled students offer insights that policy documents and institutional reports often miss. These students not only name the barriers they encounter; they illuminate how systems fail and where transformation is most needed. Their reflections serve as a roadmap for building institutions that center equity, not just access.

This chapter is not intended to generalize or universalize the experience of disability in higher education. Each narrative included here is shaped by multiple and intersecting identities: race, gender, sexuality, class, language, and more. Students speak from different geographies, educational pathways, and support systems. What they share, however, is the reality of navigating institutions that were not designed with them in mind. Their stories call attention to the cumulative toll of being required to advocate constantly, justify one's needs, and endure isolation while striving for academic and personal growth.

Centering disabled voices is a political act. It resists the tendency of institutions to speak for disabled students without speaking with them. It pushes back against deficit-based narratives that portray disabled learners as burdens rather than experts in adaptation and innovation. By listening deeply, we do not simply affirm their humanity, we learn what equity truly demands. We are reminded that policy alone does not change culture. Stories do. As we move through this chapter, each section presents testimonies that correspond to the structural themes explored in previous chapters, access, identity, technology, relationships, and vision. Together, these narratives are not just reflections. They are demands. They call us to recognize that transforming postsecondary education begins with listening, and that listening must lead to action.

Pseudonyms are used throughout this chapter to protect the privacy of the individuals whose stories are shared. These narratives are based on real experiences and are presented with consent, care, and a commitment to honoring each student's truth.

Section 1: Navigating Access and Inaccessibility

For many students with disabilities, the journey to and through higher education is marked by a constant struggle for access. Access is often framed as a matter of accommodation, extra time on tests, note-taking assistance, or alternative formats. But these supports, when delivered without care, timeliness, or respect, can reinforce exclusion rather than disrupt it. Students often find themselves having to prove their disability, negotiate their needs repeatedly, or wait weeks for basic services. These barriers are not the result of resource constraints alone; they are the product of ableist assumptions about who belongs in academic spaces and who must adjust to be included.

Elena, a first-generation Latinx student with a chronic illness, described her first semester as a series of battles. "I applied for accommodations before classes even started," she said, "but I didn't get a response until week five. By then I had already failed a midterm." Her story reflects a pattern many students know too well: bureaucratic delays that lead to academic consequences. She spoke of emailing professors only to be ignored, or told to "just keep up." Her illness flared under stress, and her sense of belonging disappeared. "I didn't need extra help. I needed someone to believe me," she said. "Access isn't about special treatment. It's about not being punished for having a body that works differently."

Other students pointed to the inaccessibility of physical spaces on campus. Ramps were steep or poorly maintained. Elevators were out of service. Automatic door openers didn't work. Jayden, a Black student who uses a wheelchair, recalled being unable to attend a study group because the designated meeting room was on the second floor of a building with no elevator. "They told me they'd fix it 'next semester,'" he said. "But my class was this semester." For Jayden, the problem was not just the inaccessible room, it was the message that his presence was optional. "It's not that they don't know we exist," he said. "It's that they don't plan for us."

Digital access presented its own challenges. Several students recounted courses that relied heavily on video content without captions, learning management systems that were incompatible with screen readers, or professors who posted scanned PDFs with no text recognition. Leila, a legally blind student, described spending hours converting materials into accessible formats, labor that her peers never had to consider. "By the time I finish preparing the material, the class has already moved on," she explained. "Accessibility shouldn't be extra credit. It should be built in." She expressed exhaustion, not from her disability, but from the constant work of compensating for institutional neglect.

What emerges from these stories is a portrait of access not as a checklist but as a culture. Access is emotional as much as it is logistical. It shapes how students feel about themselves, their place in the institution, and their right to be there. When denied access, students are not only blocked from content, they are sent a message about their worth. But when access is intentional, anticipatory, and affirming, it becomes a source of possibility. As the testimonies in this section reveal, the difference between surviving and thriving in college often hinges not on a student's capacity, but on an institution's willingness to listen, adapt, and care.

Section 2: Identity, Intersectionality, and Belonging

Disability does not operate alone. For many students, it intersects with race, gender identity, socioeconomic status, language background, and more, shaping how they are seen, supported, and silenced within higher education. These overlapping identities do not simply add layers of complexity; they create unique contexts of oppression and resilience. Students with multiple marginalized identities often experience exclusion in ways that are harder to name and easier to dismiss. Their stories challenge higher education's tendency to view students through single-issue lenses and instead demand a more holistic, justice-centered understanding of identity.

Malik, a Black autistic student, described how his behaviors in class were frequently misread. "If I didn't make eye contact, they said I was disengaged. If I spoke up too often, I was disruptive. If I didn't speak at all, I wasn't participating," he shared. Malik's professors often failed to recognize the cultural and neurological frameworks that shaped his communication. "I was always too much or not enough," he said. "But never just right." His story reflects a broader pattern: how Black students with disabilities are often hyper-surveilled, misunderstood, and penalized, not because of lack of ability, but because of institutionalized racism and ableism operating simultaneously.

Other students described being caught between cultural expectations and institutional demands. Amina, a first-generation immigrant student with an anxiety disorder, shared how her family discouraged her from seeking accommodations. "They didn't think mental health was a real issue," she said. "They told me to just pray about it and stay strong." When she finally approached her disability services office, she was met with paperwork, long waitlists, and a tone that made her feel like a burden. "I almost gave up. It was like I had to fight two battles, one at home, and one at school," she reflected. Her experience underscores the importance of culturally responsive disability support that acknowledges diverse belief systems and lived realities.

Trans and nonbinary students also spoke about the compounded impact of gender identity and disability. Alex, a neurodivergent student who uses they/them pronouns, shared how exhausting it was to constantly educate others. "I had to explain my pronouns, explain my access needs, and explain why I didn't want to be grouped into either male or female in classroom discussions," they said. "It wasn't just draining, it was erasing." They noted that while some professors were supportive, many failed to challenge binary norms or incorporate inclusive practices. "I didn't want special treatment. I wanted to be respected." For students like Alex, inclusion means being seen in the fullness of their identities, not having to fragment themselves for acceptance.

Belonging was a recurring theme across all narratives. For some students, it was found in disability cultural centers, affinity groups, or relationships with faculty who affirmed their whole selves. For others, belonging remained elusive, something they felt they had to earn by minimizing parts of who they were. What these students made clear is that intersectionality is not a theory to be quoted in classrooms, it is a lived condition that shapes every academic interaction, every policy, and every perception of worth. Postsecondary institutions must understand that equity requires more than access ramps and learning accommodations. It requires the active creation of spaces where disabled students of color, queer disabled students, and others with intersecting identities are not merely included, but fully embraced.

Section 3: Technology, Tools, and Transformation

Technology is often celebrated as the great equalizer in education, particularly for students with disabilities. Digital tools can remove physical barriers, provide multiple means of engagement, and support personalized learning. But for many disabled students, access to technology is inconsistent, frustrating, and burdened with hidden labor. When institutions fail to provide appropriate training, compatible platforms, or timely support, the promise of technology becomes another site of inequity. In the lived experiences of students, technology is not inherently empowering, it becomes empowering only when systems and structures make it so.

Tariq, a low-income student with a learning disability, recalled how the campus's assistive technology lab became a lifeline, but only after months of delay. "No one told me it existed. I found out through another student," he said. "By then I had already failed two quizzes because I couldn't use the reading software at home." Once he accessed the tools he needed, text-to-speech software and digital annotation programs, his academic confidence improved. But the damage to his GPA and self-esteem had already been done. "I didn't need a miracle," he said. "I just needed the tools in time." His story reflects the systemic disconnect between availability and accessibility: Tools may exist, but without guidance and outreach, students are left to fend for themselves.

Some students found liberation in technology, especially when it enabled independence and creative expression. Jasmine, a deaf student majoring in media studies, described how video editing software and captioning tools helped her thrive. "I could tell stories on my terms," she said. "Technology gave me a voice that didn't rely on speech." Yet she was quick to point out that this empowerment came in spite of, not because of, her university's infrastructure. "The school didn't provide the software, I saved up and bought it myself. They told me to just use the free version, even though it didn't meet my needs." For Jasmine, the gap between institutional rhetoric about inclusion and the practical realities of digital access was glaring.

Surveillance-based technologies emerged as a common point of concern. Students described the stress of remote proctoring tools that misinterpreted their behavior, flagging involuntary movements, perceived "eye diversion," or background noise as evidence of cheating. Andre, a student with Tourette's syndrome, explained how the software repeatedly paused his test. "Every time I had a tic, it thought I was cheating. I had to restart the exam twice," he said. "By the end, I wasn't focused on the material, I was just trying not to move." His experience echoes the harms described in Chapter 8:

Technologies that prioritize compliance over understanding often exacerbate exclusion.

Students also reflected on the emotional toll of being constantly required to advocate for access to technology. Many shared that when they asked professors for accessible file formats or captioned content, their requests were met with confusion, delay, or outright refusal. This burden fell especially hard on students from historically marginalized communities, who already faced barriers to being heard. When institutions failed to anticipate access needs, students were left to carry the additional labor of explaining, reminding, and justifying their needs, often at the expense of their academic focus and well-being.

Yet amid these challenges, students also described moments of possibility, when technology was intuitive, integrated, and affirming. These moments were often made possible not by policy alone, but by relationships: a faculty member who asked what tools worked best, a tech specialist who offered one-on-one support, or a peer who shared access tips in a group chat. These small but meaningful interventions reveal what is possible when institutions treat technology not as a generic solution, but as a site of collaboration, care, and inclusion.

Section 4: Relationships, Community, and Resistance

Success in higher education is not just determined by academic ability or access to accommodations, it is deeply shaped by relationships. For disabled students, connection can be the difference between isolation and survival, between invisibility and belonging. Yet many students enter postsecondary spaces where they feel alone in their experiences, misunderstood by faculty, and unsupported by peers. Despite this, they often create their own networks of care, resistance, and advocacy. These relationships form the backbone of resilience, not because institutions are doing enough, but because students refuse to give up on themselves or each other.

Isaiah, a blind student in a large STEM program, shared how peer mentorship helped him navigate a program that was not built with accessibility in mind. "None of the lab materials were screen reader friendly. I had to rely on classmates just to complete basic assignments," he said. While his department offered no formal solutions, Isaiah and a fellow student began developing alternative materials together. "He wasn't disabled, but he cared. He took the time to learn what I needed." That relationship didn't just improve his grades, it shifted his sense of what was possible. "He made me feel like I belonged in that lab," Isaiah said. "Not just as a student, but as a scientist."

Faculty relationships also shaped students' sense of inclusion. When professors believed in their students, adapted their teaching, and invited honest dialogue, the impact was profound. Nia, a student with bipolar disorder, recalled a professor who reached out after she missed several classes. "She didn't accuse me of slacking off. She just said, 'I noticed you haven't been yourself. Do you want to talk about how we can support you?'" That moment of care helped Nia re-engage with the class and reconnect with her sense of purpose. "She treated me like a person, not a problem. That made all the difference." Her story illustrates that disability inclusion is not always about policy, it's about presence, empathy, and the willingness to listen.

Yet many students also spoke of being misunderstood, judged, or excluded by faculty and peers. Anthony, a Latinx student with ADHD, described being labeled "lazy" by a professor who refused to honor his accommodations. "He said if I couldn't meet deadlines, maybe college wasn't for me," Anthony said. That dismissal stung not only because it was inaccurate, but because it echoed years of being told he was incapable. In response, Anthony joined a student-led disability justice group where he found affirmation, tools, and a space to share his story. "We organized panels, pushed for policy changes, and supported each other when no one else would. We made our presence felt."

These collective spaces, formal and informal, often serve as incubators of resistance. Students spoke about sharing resources through group chats, crowdsourcing lecture notes, and using social media to hold institutions accountable. In these communities, disability was not pathologized but celebrated as a site of knowledge and culture. Jasmine, who identified as queer and autistic, explained, "It was the first time I didn't have to explain why I needed something. People just got it." These spaces allowed students to rest, to laugh, to grieve, and to strategize. "We weren't just surviving," she said. "We were building something better."

Relationships are not a luxury in higher education, they are essential infrastructure. When institutions neglect to foster meaningful connection, students often take on the work themselves, forming communities that become both shield and sword. These communities are not just sources of emotional support, they are engines of institutional change. They model what postsecondary education could look like if equity and care were truly embedded at every level.

Section 5: Reimagining the Future of Postsecondary Education

While much of this chapter has focused on the barriers students face, their narratives also carry visions—bold, grounded, and deeply hopeful—about what postsecondary education could become. These visions are not utopian dreams; they are informed by daily experiences of exclusion and the radical imagining that survival requires. Students with disabilities are not waiting for change to happen; they are articulating what justice looks like, often more clearly than the institutions around them. Their reflections challenge us to move beyond technical compliance and toward a reimagined future built on accountability, creativity, and care.

Camille, a student with a physical disability, spoke of a campus culture where she no longer had to preface every request with an apology. "I imagine a school where I don't have to prove I deserve to be here every semester," she said. "Where access isn't a favor, it's a foundation." Her dream was not about receiving more accommodations, but about being part of a university where accessibility was universal, where buildings, syllabi, websites, and classroom norms reflected an assumption of human diversity. "In the future I want," she added, "students like me don't get thanked for our patience. We get supported because it's the bare minimum."

Other students envisioned a shift in pedagogy and faculty engagement. Omar, a neurodivergent student, spoke about classrooms that prioritize flexibility, multimodal learning, and relationship building.

"I want professors who see learning differences as part of the classroom's design, not as disruptions to it," he said. "A future where we stop pretending that one way of teaching works for everyone." He imagined a world where faculty training included disability justice, where professors didn't just receive memos from disability services, but co-created learning plans with students. His vision was not only about improving academic outcomes, it was about transforming who gets to define rigor, success, and belonging.

Several students called for a redefinition of inclusion beyond access checklists. For them, inclusion meant visibility: seeing disabled faculty in leadership, having disability studies courses across disciplines, and celebrating disability culture on campus. Aaliyah, a student with multiple disabilities, said, "I want to see my story reflected in the curriculum, not as a problem, but as history, as literature, as resistance." She spoke of events that center disabled artists, peer-led advocacy trainings, and student unions that affirm cross-disability solidarity. "In my future campus," she said, "disability isn't hidden. It's everywhere. And it's powerful."

Table 9.1 highlights key insights and demands that emerged across student narratives, reflecting a shared vision for systemic reform grounded in lived experience. Students also demanded changes in accountability and resource allocation. They wanted institutions to collect and publish data on access gaps, invest in accessible technology from the start, and ensure that disabled students had decision-making power in university governance. "If you're not tracking how disabled students are doing, by race, income, gender, all of it, you're not doing equity work," said DeShawn, a Black student with a psychiatric disability. He envisioned performance evaluations for administrators that include accessibility metrics, budgets that reflect disability equity as a priority, and complaint processes that result in actual change. "Don't say inclusion matters. Show me where the money goes," he said. "That's how we'll know you mean it."

Table 9.1 – Key Themes From Student Narratives on Postsecondary Transition

Theme	Description	Implications for Practice
Navigating Invisibility	Students felt overlooked or misunderstood in both high school and college	Institutions must recognize diverse disability identities and communicate proactively
Power of Early Advocacy	Those who learned to self-advocate in high school transitioned more confidently	Early instruction in rights and advocacy must be embedded in transition services
Importance of Mentorship	Support from educators or peers with disabilities shaped success trajectories	Mentorship programs should prioritize cultural and disability identity matching
Barriers to Access	Students encountered inconsistent accommodations and inaccessible systems	Colleges must streamline accommodation processes and audit physical/digital spaces
Resilience and Agency	Despite challenges, students demonstrated perseverance and self-determination	Transition planning must center student voice and affirm disability pride

Listening Toward Liberation: A Call to Transform

As this chapter concludes, the imperative is clear: Listening to students with disabilities must become a foundational practice in shaping postsecondary education, not as a symbolic gesture, but as an ongoing and institutionalized responsibility. These narratives expose the systemic inequities that persist in colleges and universities, while offering vivid, grounded visions for what justice could look like. The stories in this chapter reveal what formal reports cannot: the labor, the exclusion, the persistence, and the brilliance of disabled students who continue to demand better. These students have not shared their truths simply to be acknowledged, they have spoken to incite transformation.

The final chapter, *Charting the Future of Postsecondary Transition*, turns to that transformation. Drawing from the lived experiences shared throughout this book, I will outline what it means to move from theory to practice, from advocacy to action, and from incrementalism to systemic change. This concluding chapter offers a roadmap, not a universal prescription, but a framework for building postsecondary systems that are just, inclusive, and sustainable. If this chapter honored the voices of those navigating the present, the one that follows seeks to imagine and build the future they deserve.

CHAPTER 10

Charting the Future of Postsecondary Transition

The Future Is Not Neutral

The future of postsecondary transition for students with disabilities will not be shaped by chance. It will be shaped by choices, by the decisions institutions, policymakers, and communities make about whose success is prioritized, whose needs are planned for, and whose voices are centered in design and accountability. The current systems, built on compliance-driven logic and deficit-based expectations, are not failing by accident, they are functioning exactly as they were structured to. To chart a new path forward requires more than reform. It demands reimagining transition as a justice-driven ecosystem, rooted in access, dignity, and collective accountability.

Across this book, I have explored the systemic barriers that disabled students face and the transformative potential of inclusive, student-centered practices. But reflection alone does not yield equity. The question that remains is not whether change is needed, it is how bold and how immediate that change must be. Postsecondary transition must move beyond accommodations delivered at the margins of an inaccessible system. It must be restructured from the ground up to anticipate, affirm, and sustain the full diversity of disability experiences.

This chapter offers a forward-facing framework for what that restructuring can look like. Drawing on student testimony, research, and institutional analysis, I outline key areas for intervention and redesign, from how readiness is defined to how interagency collaboration is funded and governed. The solutions offered here are not exhaustive, but they are strategic and grounded in practice. They are designed to challenge inertia and push systems toward meaningful transformation. This is the final chapter of the book, but it is not the end of the work. Transition equity must be treated not as a special initiative or a legal requirement, but as a defining measure of institutional integrity. The choices made today, about policy, design, funding, and power, will shape not only who transitions successfully, but who gets to dream freely. The future is not neutral. It must be built with intention, and it must begin now.

Redefining Readiness Through Equity

For too long, college and career readiness has been defined through narrow, ableist frameworks. Metrics like standardized test scores, GPA, and behavioral conformity dominate readiness evaluations, positioning success as something to be measured in compliance rather than in capacity. These measures often ignore or penalize the very students most in need of systemic support: those navigating disability, poverty, racism, language marginalization, and trauma. When institutions fail to interrogate how these definitions of readiness are constructed, they reinforce exclusion rather than challenge it.

Readiness must be redefined not as a static condition but as a dynamic, relational process. It is shaped not only by a student's preparation, but by the system's ability to support diverse needs. Equity-focused definitions of readiness should recognize strengths such as self-advocacy, adaptability, cultural identity awareness, problem-solving, and community engagement, skills that many disabled students develop through lived experience. These are not secondary traits; they are central to navigating adulthood, higher education, and the workforce. They must be integrated into how readiness is assessed and supported.

This redefinition also requires a shift in language and assumptions. Terms like "not ready," "low functioning," or "behind" are often reflections of institutional inflexibility, not of a student's capability. Instead of asking whether a student can survive in a traditional postsecondary setting, the better question is: What structures and relationships must be in place for this student to thrive? A justice-centered approach resists deficit thinking and instead asks how to transform the system itself to ensure alignment with each student's goals, strengths, and identities.

Building this new readiness paradigm involves co-constructing success metrics with students themselves. Students must be asked how they define their goals, what success looks like to them, and what supports they need to achieve it. Transition planning teams, educational leaders, and policymakers must engage in collaborative conversations that honor student agency and disrupt imposed hierarchies of ability and worth. Redefining readiness in this way is not only more equitable, it is more accurate, more humane, and more responsive to the diversity of learners in today's classrooms and campuses.

Embedding Disability Justice in Institutional Policy

Justice in postsecondary transition requires more than inclusive intentions, it demands structural accountability. Too often, schools and colleges treat disability as an individual issue, addressing needs through accommodations rather than reexamining the systems that create inaccessibility in the first place. While policies such as the Individuals with Disabilities Education Act (IDEA) and the Americans with Disabilities Act (ADA) have laid critical groundwork, they are frequently implemented in ways that emphasize compliance over transformation. Disability becomes a matter of checklists and forms, rather than an opportunity to interrogate whose needs are centered in institutional design.

Embedding disability justice into policy begins with a shift in institutional priorities. Postsecondary systems must explicitly name disability equity as a strategic imperative, integrating it into mission statements, accreditation frameworks, budget decisions, and leadership evaluations. Equity goals must be reflected not only in access offices, but across departments, from curriculum development and residential life to admissions and academic advising. Transition planning cannot be isolated from these systems; it must be a coordinated, university-wide responsibility anchored in inclusive values.

Accountability must also be measurable. Institutions should disaggregate transition outcome data by race, disability category, language background, gender identity, and socioeconomic status. Without disaggregation, inequity remains hidden. With it, patterns become visible and actionable. Publicly sharing this data allows communities to monitor progress, challenge disparities, and advocate for targeted solutions. Reporting must go beyond enrollment numbers and include metrics related to persistence, sense of belonging, post-graduation employment, and access to disability services. Numbers cannot tell the whole story, but they are necessary tools in making institutions answerable to the students they serve.

Another critical policy intervention involves the inclusion of disabled students in governance. Equity cannot be legislated without lived experience at the table. Institutions must create advisory bodies, leadership pathways, and compensated roles that position students with disabilities as co-creators of transition strategy and campus life. When policy is developed without those most affected by it, the result is often inefficiency at best and exclusion at worst. Centering student voice is not an optional gesture, it is an ethical and operational necessity.

Disability justice requires institutions to move beyond access as a goal and toward equity as a practice. That shift is only possible when disability is seen not as a problem to be managed, but as a vital dimension of diversity to be celebrated and engaged. When institutional policy reflects this understanding, transition becomes more than a service, it becomes a shared, structural commitment to ensuring that every student is prepared not just to enter higher education, but to thrive within it and beyond.

Reimagining the Transition Ecosystem

Postsecondary success does not begin on the first day of college, nor does it exist in isolation from K-12 schooling, community systems, or family life. Transition must be understood as a process that spans multiple institutions, timelines, and spheres of influence. Yet in practice, the systems intended to support students with disabilities often operate in silos, school districts disconnected from colleges, colleges disconnected from employers, and families left to navigate these gaps alone. Reimagining transition requires breaking down these walls and constructing a coordinated, justice-centered ecosystem of support.

This ecosystem must be built on cross-sector collaboration. Schools, colleges, vocational rehabilitation agencies, healthcare providers, housing services, transportation systems, and community-based organizations all have roles to play in creating a seamless postsecondary transition experience. When these systems communicate and collaborate, students are more likely to access consistent support, avoid service disruption, and maintain progress toward their goals. Coordination should be more than a memorandum of understanding; it should be woven into policy, planning, and funding streams.

Effective interagency collaboration also requires shared accountability. Too often, no single entity takes responsibility for transition outcomes, allowing students to fall through the cracks. Each agency must be held accountable for specific, measurable contributions to the student's transition plan. This includes clearly defined roles, timelines, data-sharing protocols, and follow-up procedures. Importantly, students and families should be at the center of this process, with full access to information and input into every decision made. When transition systems are responsive and transparent, they empower, rather than overwhelm, the young people they are meant to serve.

Community partnerships play a vital role in expanding what transition can offer. Nonprofits, youth programs, advocacy groups, and local businesses bring expertise, cultural knowledge, and flexible models of support that formal institutions often lack. These partners can provide mentorship, accessible internships, supported employment, and housing navigation, elements that are often essential to successful adulthood but beyond the scope of traditional schooling. Collaboration must be resourced and sustained, not left to individual initiative. Institutions should invest in these partnerships through shared staffing, funding agreements, and long-term planning.

A justice-centered transition ecosystem acknowledges that disabled students do not simply need to be handed off from one system to the next, they need continuity, consistency, and care. The goal is not simply to move students from school to college or work, but to build a supportive infrastructure that remains with them throughout their journey. This requires dismantling institutional silos, redistributing power, and co-creating systems that reflect the realities and aspirations of disabled youth. Transition cannot be the responsibility of one office or one educator, it must be the shared, ongoing work of an entire community.

Investing in People, Not Just Programs

Too often, efforts to improve transition outcomes for students with disabilities focus on programs, new curricula, initiatives, or toolkits, without addressing the people who are charged with enacting them. Transition systems are only as effective as the professionals who design, deliver, and sustain them. Yet many educators, disability services staff, advisors, and administrators are underprepared to support the full diversity of students they serve. Investing in high-quality, justice-driven professional development is essential if transition systems are to move from compliance to transformation.

This investment must begin with the recognition that technical knowledge alone is not enough. Professionals supporting disabled students need cultural competence, trauma-informed practices, and a deep understanding of how race, disability, gender, class, and language intersect to shape educational experiences. A teacher may know how to complete a transition plan form, but without the capacity to engage in asset-based conversations about student identity and goals, that plan is unlikely to reflect the student's true aspirations. Professional development must prioritize reflection, empathy, and critical inquiry, not just procedural knowledge.

Institutions must also ensure that staff roles related to transition are clearly defined, adequately resourced, and treated as essential, not ancillary. In many districts and campuses, transition responsibilities are fragmented across multiple individuals with little coordination or support. Transition specialists are often overwhelmed, general educators may lack training, and disability services offices are underfunded. Investing in people means providing time for collaboration, reasonable caseloads, mentorship opportunities, and compensation that reflects the importance of the work.

A truly inclusive transition system must also include disabled professionals in every layer of leadership and service. Students need to see themselves reflected in the adults who support them. Hiring, retaining, and promoting educators, advisors, and administrators with disabilities affirms the value of lived experience as expertise and expands institutional knowledge of disability. Pipeline programs, leadership development, and mentorship initiatives can support disabled professionals in accessing and sustaining roles in education. Institutions must be intentional about eliminating barriers to employment, from inaccessible hiring processes to punitive leave policies that disproportionately affect disabled workers.

Professional learning cannot be a one-time training or checkbox activity. It must be embedded in the culture of an institution, woven into faculty meetings, staff onboarding, program reviews, and leadership evaluations. It should be ongoing, collaborative, and responsive to student and community feedback. Transition is human work, and justice in transition requires that the people doing that work are equipped, supported, and committed to equity at every level.

Designing With, Not For

A truly equitable transition system cannot be built for students without students. Yet in many educational spaces, transition planning is treated as a professional task, conducted by adults with little meaningful involvement from the young people whose lives are being shaped. Students are too often asked to sign forms, attend meetings, or answer prewritten questions, without being invited to define what success looks like for themselves. This approach not only disempowers students, it results in transition plans and supports that fail to reflect their lived realities, identities, or ambitions. To chart a more just future, institutions must commit to designing with, not for, disabled students.

Participatory design begins by honoring student voice as a form of expertise. Students should be engaged as collaborators in planning, evaluation, and decision-making processes. This means involving them in everything from individual transition meetings to institutional committees, program audits, and policy development. It also means creating space for students to critique existing systems, propose new models, and lead initiatives. Student participation must be accessible, compensated, and respected, not tokenized or extracted. When students are treated as partners, not passive recipients, transition systems become more responsive, more authentic, and more effective.

Universal Design for Learning (UDL) provides one framework for building inclusivity into transition systems. UDL encourages the development of flexible learning environments that anticipate variability and center accessibility from the beginning, rather than retrofitting accommodations after the fact. But UDL must extend beyond the classroom and into advising, work-based learning, assessments, and student services. Designing systems that welcome all students requires a shift in institutional thinking, from responding to needs to planning for them. This proactive mindset transforms the role of educators and administrators from gatekeepers to architects of equity.

Designing with students also means recognizing the cultural and intersectional dimensions of disability. Transition plans should reflect a student's racial, linguistic, gender, and familial context, not erase it. Institutions must ensure that transition tools and processes are inclusive of multilingual learners, LGBTQ+ students, and students with multiple disabilities. This may involve translated materials, gender-inclusive options, accessible digital platforms, and culturally sustaining pedagogies. The goal is not simply to accommodate difference, but to value it as central to the design of effective transition practices.

When systems are designed with disabled students, when their perspectives guide structure, policy, and pedagogy, education becomes not just more inclusive, but more transformative. Co-creation shifts power, builds trust, and leads to solutions grounded in lived experience. It affirms that transition is not about getting students ready for institutions, but about getting institutions ready for students. Justice begins when design is participatory, relational, and accountable to those most impacted.

Policy Recommendations and Action Steps

Creating a more just and effective postsecondary transition system requires more than visionary language, it demands concrete, enforceable action at every level of the education landscape. Policy is a powerful lever, and when wielded with intention, it can reshape the conditions that enable or deny opportunity. The following recommendations offer a strategic framework for transforming transition policy from a set of procedural mandates into a living, equity-centered practice.

First, institutions must be required to collect and report disaggregated postsecondary outcome data. Transition success rates should be publicly available and broken down by disability category, race, language background, gender identity, and socioeconomic status. Data transparency is a necessary condition for accountability. Without it, systemic inequities remain obscured, and communities have no means to demand improvement. This data should include not only enrollment and graduation rates, but also measures such as access to accommodations, campus climate experiences, retention, and employment outcomes.

Second, states and school districts must embed transition equity into strategic planning processes and performance frameworks. Transition planning should not be relegated to a single IEP meeting or office. It should be woven into district-wide equity goals, leadership evaluations, and institutional resource allocation. Schools should be evaluated not only on whether transition plans exist, but on the quality of student involvement, alignment with student strengths and goals, and long-term outcomes. When transition becomes a cross-departmental responsibility, it gains both visibility and effectiveness.

Third, funding structures must shift to reflect the complexity of high-quality transition services. Schools and postsecondary institutions require sustained investments to implement inclusive practices, build interagency partnerships, train staff, and support students holistically. Federal and state budgets should provide targeted grants for justice-centered transition initiatives, including programs led by disabled students and community organizations. Funding should not reward minimal compliance, it should prioritize innovation, collaboration, and impact.

Fourth, students and families must be given mechanisms to advocate for change and demand redress. Accessible complaint procedures, family advocacy networks, and student advisory councils should be required at both the secondary and postsecondary levels. These mechanisms must be protected from retaliation and embedded within institutional cultures that welcome critique. When students are able to challenge harmful practices and help shape solutions, transition becomes a shared responsibility rather than a bureaucratic burden.

Finally, all professionals involved in transition must be held to clear, equity-aligned standards of practice. Licensure requirements, professional development mandates, and institutional policies should include competencies in culturally responsive pedagogy, disability justice, and collaborative planning. Systems must prioritize not just who is served, but how they are served, ensuring that transition support is grounded in dignity, self-determination, and high expectations for all students.

These policy recommendations are not exhaustive, but they reflect a broader truth: Justice in transition is not optional. It must be planned for, invested in, and measured with intention. When institutions shift from viewing transition as a formality to treating it as a right, the impact ripples far beyond graduation.

Imagining the Future and Committing to It

The work of postsecondary transition has always been about more than logistics or paperwork; it is about futures. It is about the futures of students who have long been told to shrink their dreams to fit narrow systems, and about the futures of institutions that have the power and the responsibility to make those systems expansive enough for everyone. The stories, strategies, and frameworks shared throughout this book reveal both the urgency and the possibility of creating educational environments where disabled students are not merely accommodated, but genuinely supported, affirmed, and seen.

The question is no longer whether transition systems are working; they are not, at least not for the students who have been most marginalized by ableism, racism, and systemic neglect. The real question is whether leaders, educators, policymakers, and communities are willing to act. To act not just out of obligation, but out of a commitment to justice. Not just for compliance, but for transformation. Disabled students are not waiting, they are organizing, advocating, imagining, and leading. The systems must now follow.

Charting the future of postsecondary transition means rejecting frameworks that view disability as a barrier to overcome and embracing models that recognize it as a powerful dimension of identity and expertise. It means designing systems that do not wait for students to fail before intervening, but that anticipate their success and invest in their growth. It means creating a culture where the question is no longer "Are they ready?" but "Is the system ready to meet them with what they need and deserve?"

The transformation of transition is not a solitary act, it is a collective commitment. It will require courage, collaboration, and the humility to unlearn what is insufficient and rebuild what is just. As this book closes, the charge remains open: to design, advocate, and lead in ways that honor the full humanity of disabled students and expand what is possible in their educational journeys. Transition is not the end. It is the beginning of everything students have been told they could not be.

AFTERWORD

ARNE DUNCAN

When I first met Antonio Ellis, he was a young scholar with a bold voice, an unwavering moral compass, and a fierce commitment to justice. As an intern in the U.S. Department of Education, Antonio brought more than insight; he brought lived experience, truth-telling, and a vision for the kind of educational system our country needs but too often fails to build. Now, years later, I am honored to offer this afterword for his transformative book, *Beyond Graduation: Navigating Postsecondary Success for Students With Disabilities*.

This book is more than a contribution to the literature on disability and education, it is a call to action. Antonio invites us to confront not only the barriers that students with disabilities face in postsecondary settings, but the deeply rooted inequities that shape how we define ability, access, and achievement in the first place. With clarity and compassion, he brings forward stories, research, and strategies that challenge the status quo and reframe our understanding of what it truly means to support students beyond high school.

Too often, postsecondary success is treated as a destination, a static outcome we measure in degrees earned or jobs secured. Antonio reminds us that success is dynamic, relational, and often hard-won for students navigating systems never designed with them in mind. Whether confronting inaccessible learning environments, implicit bias, or the absence of culturally responsive support, students with disabilities carry burdens that too few institutions acknowledge. Antonio does not shy away from this truth. Instead, he leans into it, amplifying the voices of students and communities who know these systems intimately and continue to resist them with resilience and ingenuity.

As Secretary of Education, I often said that education is the civil rights issue of our time. But Antonio's work pushes that claim even further; it challenges us to consider whose civil rights we fight for, and whether we have the courage to confront the intersections of race, disability, language, and class that complicate our efforts. *Beyond Graduation* is grounded in justice, but it is also deeply personal. Antonio's journey, as a Black man with a stuttering disability, as an educator, as a scholar, and as an advocate, infuses every page. That lived experience gives this book its power. It is not written from the margins, it is written from the frontlines.

One of the things that moved me most as I read this book is Antonio's insistence on reframing support not as charity, but as justice. He does not ask for accommodations to be offered out of compliance, but out of a belief in the dignity and brilliance of every student. He challenges colleges, universities, and workforce programs to recognize their responsibility, not only to include students with disabilities, but to transform their systems in ways that affirm and uplift those students from the beginning. That is how we shift from reactive to proactive, from transactional to transformational.

This book is also full of practical wisdom. From transition planning to assistive technology, from faculty preparation to campus climate, Antonio offers insights that are both research informed and community grounded. He bridges the worlds of policy, practice, and lived experience with rare skill. Educators will learn from this book. Policymakers should listen to it. And students, especially those who have felt unseen or unheard, will find themselves within its pages.

But Antonio also reminds us that no single book, policy, or program is enough. What's needed is a sustained commitment, across institutions and across time, to build a postsecondary system where students with disabilities don't just survive, but thrive. That means investing in people, practices, and partnerships that center equity. It means training faculty and staff to understand disability as a facet of diversity, not a deficit. It means creating pathways that are flexible, inclusive, and responsive to the real-world challenges students face. And most of all, it means listening, truly listening, to students.

As I reflect on Antonio's journey from intern to author, I am filled with pride and hope. Pride in the scholar, advocate, and educator he has become. Hope for the future he is helping to build, one where students with disabilities are no longer left to "navigate" alone, but are equipped, supported, and celebrated at every step of the way.

Beyond Graduation is a roadmap. It is also a mirror, inviting us to look honestly at who we are and who we must become if we are to fulfill the promise of education for all.

To Antonio: Thank you for your voice, your vision, and your relentless pursuit of justice. To every reader of this book: The work continues. Let us rise to the challenge.

Antonio Ellis and Secretary Arne Duncan, 2010

Arne Duncan
Former U.S. Secretary of Education

APPENDICES

Transition Planning Checklists

The following checklists are designed to guide students, families, educators, and transition teams through essential steps and considerations in preparing for postsecondary success. They can be adapted to fit individual needs and updated annually during IEP or transition meetings.

Grades 7–8: Early Planning

Begin discussions about future goals and interests. Introduce the concept of transition planning during IEP meetings. Explore career interest inventories and learning style assessments. Identify potential mentors, role models, and support networks. Ensure inclusive access to general education settings and extracurricular activities.

Grades 9–10: Exploration and Skill Building

Conduct age-appropriate transition assessments. Develop measurable postsecondary goals within the IEP. Enroll in courses aligned with career or college aspirations. Learn self-advocacy and communication skills. Connect with disability support staff in postsecondary programs.

Grades 11–12: Decision-Making and Application

Finalize postsecondary goals and related service needs. Request copies of evaluations and records for future use. Tour colleges, training programs, or job sites. Apply for accommodations, scholarships, or financial aid. Create a transition portfolio with key documents and plans.

Postsecondary Transition (Ages 18–21 If Applicable)

Participate in work-based learning, internships, or campus bridge programs. Engage in community-based instruction focused on independent living. Coordinate services with adult agencies such as vocational rehabilitation, social security, or housing supports. Practice using accommodations in real-world settings. Review and revise goals regularly based on new insights.

Resources for Students, Families, and Educators

National Organizations and Support Networks

PACER Center (www.pacer.org): Advocacy and training for families and youth. National Technical Assistance Center on Transition (www.transitionta.org): Best practices, toolkits, and research. AHEAD (Association on Higher Education and Disability): Resources for disability services professionals and college students. Think College (www.thinkcollege.net): Inclusive higher education programs for students with intellectual disabilities. Office for Civil Rights (www.ed.gov/ocr): Guidance on rights and complaints under ADA and Section 504.

Online Tools and Portals

CareerOneStop (www.careeronestop.org): Career exploration and training locator. DO-IT (www.washington.edu/doit): Technology access and postsecondary success for students with disabilities. ADA National Network (adata.org): Regional centers providing training and legal guidance. Understood.org: Accessible resources for families navigating IEPs and college accommodations.

State and Local Resources

State vocational rehabilitation agencies. Parent Training and Information Centers. Local education agencies and transition coordinators. University disability resource centers and transition liaisons. Regional centers for assistive technology access.

Sample Accommodations Requests and Advocacy Templates

Sample Email to Request College Accommodations

Subject: Request for Disability Support Services Intake Appointment

Dear [Disability Services Coordinator's Name],

My name is [Student Name], and I will be enrolling at [College Name] in the upcoming semester. I have an IEP/504 Plan and would like to schedule a meeting to discuss potential accommodations that can support my academic success. I have documentation of my disability and am ready to submit any forms you may require. Thank you for your time and assistance. I look forward to working with your office.

Sincerely,

[Student Name][Contact Information]

Sample Self-Advocacy Script for IEP or Transition Meeting

I want to share what's important to me. After high school, I plan to [describe goal], and I would like support to help me get there. These are some accommodations that have worked for me. I'd also like to learn how to advocate for myself more when I'm on my own. I hope we can create a plan that includes my goals and makes sure I'm included in decisions.

Letter of Support for Disability Services Appeal

Dear [Office or Committee Name],

I am writing to formally request a reconsideration of my denied accommodation request for [specific need]. My disability significantly impacts my ability to [function], and the requested support is essential for equal access. I have attached updated documentation and am happy to meet for further discussion. I hope the office will honor my right to appropriate accommodations under ADA and Section 504.

Sincerely,

[Student Name]

[Student ID or Contact Info]

ABOUT THE AUTHOR

Dr. Antonio L. Ellis is a Senior Professorial Lecturer and Director of the Summer Institute on Education Equity and Justice (SIEEJ) at the American University School of Education. He teaches special education courses, advises students in the educational policy and leadership doctoral program, and supports doctoral dissertations. Dr. Ellis received his doctoral degree in educational leadership and policy studies from Howard University. He holds additional academic degrees in educational administration, theological studies, higher education, and special education and human development. He has published multiple books, including *Ed.D. Programs as Incubators for Social Justice Leadership; Transitioning Children with Disabilities: From Early Childhood through Adulthood;* and *Teacher Educators as Critical Storytellers.* He has served as an inclusion teacher, central office administrator, and school building administrator with the District of Columbia Public Schools. In addition to his practitioner work in K-12 settings, Dr. Ellis served as an adjunct professor in the College of Charleston Teacher Education Department and the Howard University School of Education Department of Educational Leadership and Policy Studies. He also served as a tenure-track assistant professor at Radford University. His passion is advocating on behalf of people with disabilities, with a special emphasis on African American males who are speech impaired. Dr. Ellis' research interests include disability studies, pastoral care, equity in higher education, Pre-K–12 educational leadership, multicultural education, critical race theory, and special education.

INDEX

S

T

U

W